SOME PHASES OF EDUCATIONAL PROGRESS IN LATIN AMERICA

First published 1920
This edition published by Lector House in 2024

ISBN: 978-93-6138-235-2

Lector House LLP
Registered Office: H. No. 96, Block C, Tomar Colony,
Burari, Delhi – 110084, India
info@lectorhouse.com
www.lectorhouse.com

SOME PHASES OF EDUCATIONAL PROGRESS IN LATIN AMERICA

WALTER ALEXANDER MONTGOMERY

2024

LECTOR HOUSE LLP

SOME PHASES OF EDUCATIONAL PROGRESS IN LATIN AMERICA

BY

WALTER A. MONTGOMERY

SPECIALIST IN FOREIGN EDUCATIONAL SYSTEMS
BUREAU OF EDUCATION

[Advance Sheets from the Biennial Survey of Education, 1916-1918]

Contents

SOME PHASES OF EDUCATIONAL PROGRESS IN LATIN AMERICA

By Walter A. Montgomery,

Specialist in Foreign Educational Systems, Bureau of Education.

Practical Education in Central America.

One of the most interesting aspects of the school situation in Central America and Panama is the important position occupied by commercial and industrial education in the courses of study of many institutions. Public men and teachers in Guatemala, Salvador, Honduras, Nicaragua, Costa Rica, and Panama have taken into account the need of offering to the new generation an education which shall be completely practical, with the purpose of turning the thoughts and energies of all the youth to fruitful service of their country.

The teaching of arts and crafts, as well as that of commerce and agriculture, was formerly not begun, as in the United States, upon the student's entering the secondary school, though there has for some time been a movement to make such instruction a part of the work of the advanced classes in the primary schools, to be continued in the liceo and the normal schools.

This universal interest in practical lines of education is a striking indication of the influences and tendencies now at work in Central America. In the different countries included under this designation there are schools and academies, workshops and laboratories, intended for the practical education of the student body. When it is remembered that the introduction of practical and industrial education in the school régime of Central America is a matter of the past few years, the progress realized is regarded as highly satisfactory. The rapid increase of the commerce of Central America, the improvement in the means of intercommunication, the travels of its people abroad, the influence of foreign elements in its territory, and the various interests thus awakened have aroused in the interior of the Republics composing it the belief that national greatness in modern times must rest upon economic and industrial foundations. The influx of foreign capital and the consequent establishment of powerful industrial enterprises have likewise emphasized the necessity of training men for work in such enterprises. The introduction of modern machinery, the increase of the different forms of the application of steam, the adoption of the inventions intended to gather up the results of labor, and numerous similar influences have given rise to a tremendous demand in this part of the continent for skilled and reliable mechanics. Central America has thus addressed itself with enthusiasm to the task of training the children of its schools for the activities of the present day.

The capitals, other important cities, and even many small towns have schools devoted to practical education, generally provided with buildings and equipment well adapted to this end. Honduras, for example, has founded a school for scientific instruction in the cultivation and preparation of tobacco and for the manufacture of cigars and cigarettes in the tobacco district around Danli. In several Provinces of the same Republic, and in Panama, where agriculture is subordinate, the Governments have founded schools for training pupils to weave hats and other objects.

The more generalized industrial schools are those of arts and crafts and the so-called practical schools for boys. Their organization presents marked differences. In some of the countries named there exist schools that receive pupils either as full or half time boarders, and offer night courses as the situation demands. In all these instruction is free. The Government generally offers a certain number of scholarships in the boarding schools for pupils approved by the different Departments or Provinces of the country. Tools, instruments, and supplies used in the schools are provided by the Government. In return the school exacts of such students certain services and thereby carries out certain work that represents a partial reimbursement for the amount spent upon their maintenance. This is the case with the schools of arts and crafts in Honduras and Panama. Some small schools of this class are maintained by means of the labor they carry on for private individuals and by the sale of the products they turn out.

These industrial schools are generally of two kinds: (1) Those in which the training in commercial subjects and in arts and crafts constitutes part of the regular course of study and (2) those devoted exclusively to the teaching of arts and crafts.

(1) In those of the first class the pupils study the ordinary subjects prescribed by the department of public instruction and devote only several hours weekly to arts and crafts. This class in its turn includes two groups of institutions. To be admitted to those of the first group the pupils must know how to read and write and apply the elementary rules of arithmetic. During the entire school year instruction is given in Spanish, geography, history, and arithmetic. The practical schools for girls and boys are generally of this kind, being especially numerous in Guatemala and Honduras. The schools conducted by the Christian Brothers in Nicaragua are also of this type. The duration of studies is from three to five years, a half day being devoted to the classes in the ordinary subjects of primary education and the other half to practical work. In the second group are comprised various institutions which require certificates from the higher elementary schools, such as the liceo and the higher colegio for women in Costa Rica, the National Institute in Salvador, the Central National Institute for Boys in Guatemala, and the normal schools in these countries and in Honduras.

(2) Of the special institutions which constitute the second category, there are to be noted two prominent instances in the schools of arts and crafts in Panama and in Honduras. In organization and purposes they are schools of mechanical arts, and not schools of manual training. Their workshops have not been established to impart general notions of manual arts or a general apprenticeship, but to train the pupils from entrance upon the line of education chosen by themselves. In these schools are taught carpentry, tanning, shoemaking, blacksmithing, cabinetmaking, electricity, installation and management of machinery, mechanics, printing and bookbinding, telegraphy, etc. All workshops in such schools are well equipped with machinery and tools.

All that has been said in regard to modern educational tendencies and influences to which boys are subject in the countries mentioned can be extended, though in less degree, to the girls and young women. Within the past few years women's sphere of action has steadily been enlarged, and has come to include not only teaching but various employments in shops and mercantile establishments. Within the next few years their instruction must be taken into account in schools of domestic training, vocational schools, practical schools, and the technical colegios. The organization and range of these institutions does not differ materially from those for boys. The vocational school for girls is essentially a school of arts and crafts in which the pupils devote themselves from entrance to the study of a special line, such as dressmaking, embroidery, millinery, and, in certain schools, cooking, washing and ironing, etc. A certificate of proficiency is granted them upon the completion of certain assigned courses. The other schools for girls before mentioned combine general subjects with the special apprenticeship in crafts upon which they enter as soon as they reach the higher classes of the primary school and which they continue into the high school and the normal school.

Guatemala.

The type of industrial education that prevails in Guatemala is the combination of general studies with special instruction in the arts and trades given in the practical schools for girls and for boys. There also exists in the capital a school of arts and crafts for women where instruction is given at the same time in the subjects of ordinary instruction. In the departments of manual arts which are largely, but not exclusively, attended by boys, are taught theoretical and practical blacksmithing, carpentry, printing, bookbinding and weaving, besides geography, history, botany, chemistry, zoology, geology, drawing, and Spanish language and literature. In the schools of Guatemala much attention is given subjects of a practical nature, with the purpose of training competent workmen and artisans. There also exist in this country a National School of Commerce, situated in the capital, and a Practical School of Commerce, at Quetzaltenango. In both cities there are schools of agriculture which admit to their first-year courses the pupils of the first year of the central normal schools. The capital possesses also a school of telegraphy, recently founded with the view to installing in it a special wireless station.

Salvador.

Arts and crafts for women, commercial subjects and mechanical arts, are generally taught in Salvador in the public schools, though their incorporation in the courses of instruction is comparatively recent. Many prominent teachers of the country have taken the pains to spread abroad the appreciation of the necessity of "enlarging the educational sphere of the State, and opening to the youth and to workmen schools where they may acquire practical knowledge of the sciences and the arts and by these means may contribute to the advancement of general intelligence in the country." In compliance with these ideas the Government has founded in Salvador a National School of Graphic Arts aiming "to aid the youth of Salvador to the acquisition of knowledge of a practical nature, and to put it in a position to be successful in the economic struggles which are the most important signs of the modern age." In this school the preference is given to the teaching of physics, mechanics, drawing, printing, lithographing, carving, bookbinding, and technical telegraphy and telephoning. Night courses are also given in this school.

In consequence of the public sentiment above mentioned, there has been opened in the National Institute of Salvador a course in commercial and economic subjects lasting three years. This course comprises the study of various modern languages, commercial law, political economy, industrial chemistry, commercial geography, bookkeeping, stenography and typewriting. The pupils in this school are required to work several hours daily for a period in the different ministerial departments before graduation. Salvador also established in 1913 a school of agriculture, with a department of animal husbandry. Two years later there was established the Technical-Practical Colegio for Girls, in which instruction in crafts for women is combined with that in general subjects.

Honduras.

Industrial instruction has attained great importance in Honduras. The School of Arts and Crafts of Tegucigalpa concerns itself chiefly with products in wood and the metals and is steadily training artisans and mechanics. There likewise exists in this city the national automobile school managed by the Government. For some years there has been in operation in Siguatepeque a school of English and of arts and crafts, in which are taught fiber weaving, carpentry, dressmaking, and embroidery. In the normal schools and in the two colegios students may choose between the commercial courses and those relating to arts and crafts. In 1915 was established a technical practical school for girls, where courses in science and in crafts for women are offered parallel with the subjects belonging to the primary schools.

Costa Rica.

Costa Rica is another of the Central American countries where practical instruction is combined with general. Five institutions of higher grade and the vocational schools for women have well-equipped workshops, laboratories, kitchens, and laundries. Of all Central American States, Costa Rica gives perhaps most attention to this special branch of instruction. It is noteworthy that manual arts and domestic science are uniformly taught in the secondary schools conjointly with the literary and purely scientific subjects.

Nicaragua.

In Nicaragua manual arts form part of the general instruction, as has been seen in the case of the normal schools conducted by the Christian Brothers. Girls receive practical instruction in the normal schools. Some years ago there was established a special school for the training of telegraph and telephone operators.

Panama.

Like Guatemala and Honduras, Panama has devoted special attention to industrial training. The School of Arts and Crafts of the City of Panama is one of the largest and best equipped of its kind. It is essentially a school for artisans and possesses sections of electricity, carpentry, cabinetmaking, printing and bookbinding, carving, foundry work, etc., its principal object being to train men for the separate industrial branches.

Panama also has a vocational school for girls in which a year's instruction is given in telegraphy, one in laundry work, two in dressmaking and embroidery, two in shorthand, two in cooking, two in millinery and flower work.

It has likewise a school of agriculture, in which is given a three years' course, for which the Government offers 30 scholarships to youths approved by local authorities. The Government has also founded from time to time specialized schools in the interior, with the object of encouraging agriculture or some other industry, such as that of the manufacture of Panama hats. Like Honduras, Panama devotes the greatest attention to special industrial schools.

For the furtherance of commercial education in Central and South America a Pan American College of Commerce, to be located at the City of Panama, is projected, under the joint auspices of the Southern Commercial Congress of the United States and the Government of the Republic of Panama. The active support of the countries of the two Americas is to be sought, and it is hoped that it may be opened on January 1, 1921, the quadricentennial year of the City of Panama, the first city to be founded by Europeans in the Western Hemisphere. The college is designed to train the youth of the two continents in practical courses of commerce, shipping, banking, and international trade relations generally.

New School Regulations in British Guiana.

The last report of the director of primary instruction in British Guiana outlines a new regulation for the common schools. In many of its parts it includes novel measures of school organization which are of interest as suggestions to other South American States for similar action. The regulations relate to the classification of schools, the minimum period of attendance, the age limit of pupils, the occupations of pupils after leaving school, school gardens, etc. As an instance of its stringent character, the regulation decrees that when any school ceases to conform to certain conditions with regard to building, installation, equipment, and health conditions, it shall be classified in B category; and if within 6 months it has not satisfied the requirements of the regulation, the authorities shall suspend the Government aid hitherto granted. It is to be noted that the primary schools of British Guiana are not directly administered by the authorities.

The school also loses its governmental aid if within two consecutive years it does not maintain a fixed minimum attendance, which varies according to the population of the locality in which it is situated. In return special aids are offered for schools that teach gardening for boys and the care of smaller children for girls from 12 to 14 years.

The greatest educational need of the colony is the establishment of technical primary schools for the instruction of boys and girls from 11 to 15 years. It is projected to establish two such schools in Georgetown in which there shall be taught, in addition to manual arts and other craft, drawing in all its branches, arithmetic and geography as related to commerce, the rudiments of experimental science, shorthand, and business correspondence. Criticism has been directed against the omission of instruction in agriculture, which is admitted to be the most necessary branch in the colony. It is, however, intended to impart agricultural instruction in special schools to be established.

Because of the fact that the majority of the pupils leave school before reaching 12 years, it is not possible to put into practice suggested plans of giving them preoccupational instruction in which they might be making a start before the end of their primary-school studies. On the other hand the traditional primary school is not adequate to give direction toward a vocational subject. Hence, to the regret of the authorities, attempts to link the primary school with the occupation of the pupil have been abandoned.

Much interest has been developed in school gardening; and about 100 gardens are annexed to primary schools, affording practical instruction to pupils in agriculture and horticulture. The Government has also established 8 model gardens, where instruction is given the pupils of neighboring schools.

Argentina.

Preliminary.

Two well-defined stages have marked the progress of national education in Argentina since 1916. The first began with the reorganization of primary instruction by act of the Federal Congress early in that year, which came about largely through the initiative and efforts of the minister of public instruction. It had long been felt that the legal system in force since 1882 was unsatisfactory, especially on the point of articulation of secondary education with the higher elementary on the one hand and with the universities on the other. Argentine educational thinkers asserted that secondary education prepared neither for practical life nor for entrance to the technical schools and the universities, inasmuch as it had remained unchanged for more than a generation, in the face of the social, economic, scientific, and ethnical changes through which the country had passed.

Together with this dissatisfaction with a special division went the conviction that governmental reform should strike deeper, and instead of busying itself with plans of reform of courses and schedules, should settle the fundamental question of what should be the nature and aims of the national secondary school. This could be done only by so modifying the prevailing system as to make it fit the needs of the school population according to their age, social conditions, and probable future. Proof that it had not so adapted itself was thought to be found in the fact that of the pupils annually completing the 4a elementary grade only 45 per cent continued into the *colegios nacionales*, as contrasted with 55 per cent who went into the 5a grade and commercial schools, while on a moderate estimate 60 per cent left with insufficient equipment for their needs as useful members of society. Furthermore, the secondary school, as organized, offered no opportunity to boys and girls of 13 and 14 years to choose the advanced courses and vocational training for which they felt an aptitude, and so to secure adequate preparation for the university studies or for advanced technical, industrial, and commercial schools.

For this lack of correlation between educational divisions it was proposed to substitute a logical and unbroken sequence. What came to be commonly accepted among education authorities as best serving this purpose was a common intermediate school of three years of an essentially practical character, carrying on general elementary instruction by means of book lessons and developing by special experiments and practical methods individual aptitudes by which to determine future training. As the basis for such a school primary education had, of course, to be modified, and after months of discussion a scheme for general modification of the entire educational fabric was outlined (1916). According to this, the primary school proper was to cover four years; the uniform middle school of the first grade one year; and the differentiated middle school of the second grade two years. Upon these were to be based the *colegios nacionales*, the normal schools, the industrial schools, the various higher special schools, and the national universities. Though marking a meritorious attempt to articulate the several divisions, the project did not work out satisfactorily in actual operation, and as a constituent part of the national system it was repealed after about a year of operation.

Illiteracy.

On a basis of population estimated (1917) at slightly more than eight millions, 725,000 were estimated to be illiterate, about 42 per cent of the school population. Illiteracy is most rife in remote Provinces of the Andes and in the Territories, sparsely settled and inhabited by people of roving habits and poorly developed industrially. Under the lead of the director general of the schools of the Province of Mendoza, a systematic campaign to eliminate illiteracy was begun in 1916. It was recognized that financial considerations made it impossible to establish the number of primary schools which would be demanded, certainly not for the many remote points where only the legal minimum of 15 or 20 illiterates were to be found. Home schools (*escuelas del hogar*) were therefore established, officially ranking as auxiliary to the already existent schools, for illiterates of 8 to 20 years, and offering as a minimum curriculum reading, writing, the four fundamental operations of arithmetic, the duties of the Argentine citizen, elements of ethics, and personal hygiene. Such schools may begin any day of the year, and with a minimum of five pupils. Any person desiring to open such a school must fulfill the following conditions:

(*a*) He must be at least 20 years of age, of good moral reputation, certified by the chief civil official of his residence.

(*b*) He must speak the national language correctly and be able to give instruction in it.

Such schools shall not be established at less distance than 5 kilometers from an established primary school supported by national, provincial, or local funds, but if the school be intended exclusively for boys from 15 to 20 years old it may be located at any point. Such schools are to be visited freely by school and civil authorities, and by persons designated by the provincial general inspectors.

Related in character to the *escuelas del hogar* of the Province are the *escuelas tutoriales*, established by national decree of 1916, applying to all the Provinces and especially to the Territories. In these schools, established at points designated by the National Council of Education, any number of children not regularly enrolled in the primary schools may be taught by private individuals who conform to the requirements of primary teachers, and by teachers regularly engaged in primary work. The latter, by special exception, receive additional compensation for such instruction. The same law also provides remuneration, to be fixed by the general council of education of the Province or Territory for all persons, not teachers, who are certificated to have taught illiterates, whether children or adults, to read and write.

Most novel of all undertakings for the wiping out of illiteracy are the traveling schools (*escuelas ambulantes*). Provided for by the original organic school law of 1884, these schools were not, because of lack of funds, put into operation until 1914. Up to that time there was a conviction that their need was insignificant by contrast with the greater problem of illiteracy in the cities, and that to scatter funds available for combating illiteracy was not prudent. How serious this mistake was appeared in 1914 when it was ascertained by systematic count that of nearly 35,000 children of the Territories not in school only 6,000 lived in towns.

Located first in Province of Catamarca, and in the mountain regions of Rio Negro and the Chubut, these schools are built of materials easily transportable, and accommodate an average of 25 pupils. Sites are selected for them which are most accessible to the largest number of children in the district. Teachers traverse such regions on foot or muleback, carrying necessary equipment for instruction, and remain four and one-half months at each place, giving instruction in reading, writing, elements of arithmetic, and hygiene. A decided advantage is found in this succinct curriculum, the average of successful study by the pupils of these schools being, it is claimed, fully on a par with that of the pupils of the nine months' primary schools, who are required to take the standard number of subjects.

Within their first two years of existence, 20 of these schools were established, as reported by the National Council of Education in December, 1916; and 12 were added in 1917. The report of the inspector general of the Province of Mendoza concluded as follows:

> This new type of school must exist for many years in Argentina to answer the needs of the actual distribution of the population, the lack of adequate means of communication, and the impossibility of maintaining fixed schools in the greater part of the zones engaged in agriculture and cattle raising. It behooves the authorities, therefore, to continue the improvement of the system in such manner that its efficiency shall be steadily greater, and that results shall amply compensate for their maintenance.

An interesting phase of social conscience is shown in the generous offer of the women pupils of the third and fourth years of the normal school at Santa Fe to instruct illiterates afternoons and nights in reading, writing, the elements of arithmetic, national language and history, and practical personal and school hygiene. This offer has been highly commended both by Argentine and foreign educators as a step toward solving the problem of illiteracy, worthy of imitation nationally and locally.

The struggle against illiteracy has been the subject of serious consideration by the executive, the chief school authorities, and the Congress. The executive has constantly urged the National Council of Education to intensify its campaigns and has cooperated by all means in his power in the steady diffusion of education. The Houses of Congress have also busied themselves especially with this grave problem. These efforts have borne fruit which, if not visible at the present time, is certainly destined to raise the level of popular education within the next few years. The authorities have judged that what is needed is the patient labor which does not require an immediate and striking solution of a most difficult problem, but is willing to continue to exercise an ever-increasing influence upon the rising generation, confident of the spread of education and enlightenment with the increase of population and the improvement in means of communication; and that it is not wise to sow schools broadcast throughout the Republic merely for the pleasure of doing something and of doing it rapidly. The success of the struggle against illiteracy, certain as it is, has its roots not in merely spending much money, but in spending money well.

Report of National Council of Education.

The progress of education in Argentina is best epitomized in the report of the National Council of Education for the four years ending December 31, 1916. The character of this council is unique in educational polity, wielding, as it does, greater powers than any similar body in countries educationally advanced, and counting in its membership some of the ablest men in the Nation. Its reports follow traditionally the line of national (the capital city), provincial, and territorial administration. When the very heterogeneous character of the population of Argentina, due to the steady stream of immigration, is taken into account, the necessity of such a central body, vested with powers of initiation and execution in primary education, is apparent. By a wise division of powers in the original organic law, the control of secondary education was left in the hands of the Provinces, with subsidies granted by the National Government, as was the right to prescribe subjects essential to nationalistic and patriotic training. Concentration of effort and power is thus secured, with national acquiescence in the official actions of the council. Its activities center naturally around the establishment of new schools and the construction of school buildings, and the training of teachers to meet the demands of modern conditions.

As a substitute for the abortive intermediate schools established in 1916, which soon proved unsatisfactory, the council decided later in that year to establish, parallel and auxiliary to the higher primary schools, one of practical arts and crafts for each sex in every district of Buenos Aires. Such schools approximated 100 in number. This type of school was designed for boys and girls not intending to proceed to higher studies, and was later to be extended to the nation at large. Its purpose and program of studies was two-fold—to complete the theoretical and higher courses of the higher primary schools with vocational, technical, and manual training, based upon and making use of the materials which were peculiarly Argentine and local in industries, commerce, art, and economics; and to lay stress throughout on nationalistic and patriotic aims. An interesting feature, common to these new schools and the continuation schools now arising in England and France, is the provision by which they operate 2 hours in the morning and 2 hours in the afternoon or night, and are to admit pupils from the fourth to the sixth grade of the primary schools, who have reached the age of 12 years. Statistics as to the success of these schools are not as yet available.

In the matter of building primary schools proper, the report of the council shows progress throughout the four years covered. A total of 62 schools, with 426 teachers and 19,563 pupils, was added to the system. Because of national economic and financial conditions prevailing half a century ago, the great majority of the primary schools began operation in private buildings, which did not conform to pedagogical or even sanitary requirements. For many years excessive rents were often paid by the State, but upon the revaluation of property in many Provinces in 1915, an economy in rents was effected, and the funds thus saved were devoted to new schools. Despite high prices of material and difficulties of labor, in December, 1916, eleven school buildings were in process of erection, at an estimated cost of $750,000, with a capacity of 22,000 pupils. According to the report of the council: "The construction of properly equipped Government primary school buildings has constituted one of the most serious problems and, therefore, one of the chief occupations of the council." It was frankly admitted, however, that, with all the efforts of the council, accommodations for children in the primary schools were still far from adequate, it being estimated on that date that 4,000 additional schools of this grade were needed for the more than 600,000 children in the capital and the Territories who, for one reason or another, were not in school.

The activity of the council continued to be marked in 1917. In April of that year, 143 new schools were decreed, 39 for the Federal Capital, 18 for the Provinces under the legal national subvention, and 86 for the Territories (30 being *escuelas ambulantes*), the Congress voting two millions in the national budget for the execution of this decree. The centralizing tendencies of South American countries in general, and the overwhelming dominance of the capital, secured for it so generous a share of this that it is estimated that in the Federal capital there will be for the first time room for all children of school age. For the poorer Provinces, and the Territories, which by the Tainez law of 1886 are absolutely dependent upon the central authority of the National Council, 250 schools of one and two rooms were assigned, but on an estimate about one-third of the children were still left unprovided with school facilities. Attention was repeatedly called to the need of a uniform and rigorously applied national law for compulsory school attendance.

During the year 1918 approximately 400 schools were established, and the council proposes to establish as many more during 1919 in the Provinces and the national Territories. The nation has taken charge of many provincial schools which the respective governments could not maintain by reason of lack of resources. The Province of Mendoza alone transferred 130 schools to the council of education during the month of August, 1918. Relative to the establishment of schools, regard has been had chiefly to the population of the districts which petitioned for them, as well as the number of children of school age, in order that the buildings may be installed in populous centers, where a constant attendance of pupils is reasonably assured.

The general plan of the council for the diffusion of primary education has not been put into practice in full, because of the lack of resources in some instances and in others because of the scarcity of building materials in the country. School equipment has been secured in various countries, supplies necessary having been purchased in the United States to the value of $350,000. The demand has been still unsatisfied, the capital city alone calling for the establishment of new schools every year, because of the increase of children of school age, and the Provinces have always been behind the necessary number of school buildings and facilities and have never reached the goal set by the authorities. An encouraging feature of the situation is that upon the completion of all the school buildings now under construction accommodations for 56,000 pupils in addition will be provided.

Peculiar attention has been given to the development of night schools by the council, 86 having been established and maintained by the council in the four years covered by the report. An admirably broadened scope was given them in the appeal issued by the council to the nation that the full purpose of such schools should be realized not only by the attendance of illiterates, but also of youths and adults "who, possessing some degree of education, are also desirous of improving that as related to the needs of their lives." All reforms and modifications of night schools have concerned themselves with this larger clientele. A further socializing of the night school is seen in the appeal of the council to proprietors, managers of factories, and employers of labor generally to encourage in every way in their power their employees to attend night schools and to offer prizes of various kinds for diligence and progress. Literature bearing on these schools was distributed free by the council.

In 1915 the council was empowered, by the terms of the will of a philanthropic resident of Buenos Aires, Don Felix Berasconi, who bequeathed for educational purposes a sum of three and a half million dollars, to proceed to the erection and establishment of an institution under State control which should give instruction in general primary, scientific, scientific-industrial, physical, and social education. A building was to be begun in 1916, planned in seven sections, conforming to the most modern pedagogical and sanitary demands, and with a capacity of more than 3,000 pupils. Designed to benefit the working people preeminently, it was to be situated in the section of the city showing the greatest proportion of them.

Responding to the general feeling of dissatisfaction with the results of primary education in the city of Buenos Aires, which has been unaffected by criticism for seven years, the council in June, 1917, sent out questionnaires to all inspectors and to the body of teachers calling for an expression of opinion as to (1) the merits and defects of the plans of studies, schedules, etc., then in force; (2) those of projected or possible programs, with additional features worthy to be incorporated; and (3) educational considerations bearing upon the problems of the schools of the capital. The answers showed encouraging grasp of the educational needs of the city, with significant unanimity as to the practical methods of working out necessary reforms. Salient points were:

1. That all programs should leave room for and be closely articulated with manual arts and domestic economy.

2. That the courses of arithmetic in the first, second, third, fourth, and fifth grades were overloaded, as were those of grammar in the fourth, geometry in the third and fifth, nature study in the second, geography in the second and fifth, singing in the second, and music.

3. That the primary school cycle should commence at 7 years and end at 12.

4. That primary courses and schedules for urban schools should be strictly differentiated from those for rural and country town schools.

5. That from October 15 to April 15 the school day should be from 7.30 to 11.30; from April 15 to September 30 from 12 to 4.

6. That the advancement of the teacher with the class merited a fair trial, the teacher remaining with the same class a minimum of two years and a maximum of three.

7. That the establishment of normal schools essentially for rural teachers was imperative.

It is recognized that the clearness and sanity of these answers had a marked effect upon the substance of the law presented to the Federal Congress in August, 1918.

Another interesting instance of the submission of a pedagogic matter to the teachers of the city of Buenos Aires is shown in the questionnaire asking their opinion as to the best method of teaching spelling, sent out by the inspector of the tenth district, to the teachers. In accordance with the answers to this, the vocabulary used in primary schools was reduced to categories corresponding to the several grades, to its difficulties, and to the actual needs of the life and dominant occupations of the quarter of the city from which the children were drawn. This step was highly commended in French educational circles as marking efficient grappling with pedagogical difficulties felt in all cities of whatsoever country.

The regulation of the medical and dental inspection of national schools, under decree of March, 1918, was noteworthy. According to this, professional inspectors, chosen by the Government, must within the first three months of each school year examine individually all children entering school for the first time, periodically inspect the school buildings and ground and the health conditions of the teaching and administrative staffs, and take all prophylactic measures deemed necessary against epidemics and contagious diseases. Such reports shall be transmitted to the medical inspector general. Dental inspection of schools is to have a prominent part. Every month the chief inspector shall assemble for report and mutual discussion all medical and dental inspectors in such territorial divisions as he shall see fit.

Of the regulations in detail promulgated by the council in 1918, the most important is that changing the school year to two divisions, the first beginning March 1 and continuing until June 30, followed by three weeks of vacation, and the second beginning July 21 and continuing until November 20, followed by the long vacation of the year. This change is regarded as conforming with climatic effects upon the health of school children and as being a step long needed.

Progress of Education in the Provinces.

Outside the scope of the National Council are the powers of the provincial councils. These are local, auxiliary, and reinforcing in character. Some of the Provinces are practically inactive on the side of primary education, contenting themselves with the provisions made in that field by the National Government. Others, however, among them Santa Fe, San Luis, Cordoba, Entre Rios, and, of course, Buenos Aires, are worthy of note and commendation for steady interest in matters educational, and in financial support of schools carried on independently of the central authority.

Progress in the Province of Santa Fe, as evidenced by the annual message of the governor of that Province for 1917, was steady, despite the need of economy in provincial finances due to conditions resulting from the World War. An increase of 14 provincial schools over the year previous and of the grades in 36 schools was noted. Two problems were kept steadily in view: The improvement in the teaching personnel, accentuated by the disclosure of the fact that more than one-third of the teachers in the provincial schools lacked teacher training, and the construction of better school buildings. It was estimated that with these from 25 to 30 per cent of additional pupils could be taught by the same teaching force.

In the Province of San Luis the general inspector of provinces reported for 1916 the establishment of 160 local associations of the national *Amigos de la Educacion*. This society, composed of parents and others interested in primary education, has for its objects the close linking of home and school, the fight against illiteracy, the promotion of good feeling and companionship between natives and immigrants, the celebration of national festivals, the securing of better primary enrollment and attendance especially by the poorer children, with the inculcation of their self-respect, and cooperation with the regional and national authorities in the safeguarding of public health.

In this Province, by volunteer organizations of teachers and others interested, local patriotic conferences were inaugurated on topics of national history, hygiene, political economy, ethics, and themes generally related to home and school matters.

In the Province of Buenos Aires school excursions have been developed and made an organic part of instruction in civic and national spirit. They have been so arranged that children in the several zones may come by personal touch to know and correspond by letter with each other. In some places participation in these excursions has been made a reward of good lessons and conduct. They are to be taken in the last 15 days of October, and children are not to remain more than 3 days in one locality. Groups of not more than 12 pupils are recommended.

In July, 1916, the council general of the Province of Buenos Aires initiated courses in the normal school for the training of teachers and graduates of the normal schools in the recognition and study of retardation and its causes, and in early correction of abnormalities most frequently met. The program of courses includes a series of 16 lessons on related medical and pedagogical topics.

Of direct bearing upon educational problems among the rural population is the project of the law recently sent by the executive of the Province of

Buenos Aires to the legislature, providing for the issuance of bonds to the amount of $45,000,000 for the expropriation of parts of the great landed estates and the division of the land thus expropriated into small tracts for the use of small farmers. Subsequent purchase under advantageous terms is to be encouraged. According to reports, the prevailing system of "arrendatorios," or small tenants for short terms, has led to so acute an agrarian unrest, with the consequent shifting and aimless wandering of an increasing element of the population, as to constitute a social and economic menace no longer to be ignored. The educational effects in the increase of illiteracy and the general retardation of primary education have been manifest.

In 1918 the Legislature of the Province of Entre Rios enacted into law a series of provisions guaranteeing the stability of the scale of salaries for teachers in provincial schools. Promotion and increase of salary were based rigorously upon merit; teachers were declared unremovable during good conduct and fitness; initial salaries were fixed as follows: (*a*) For normal teacher, $160 per month; (*b*) for rural normal teacher, $120 per month; (*c*) for rural teacher, $100 per month; (*d*) for special teacher, $80 per month. Every five years the teacher who has worked in the same place for that period shall receive a bonus of 20 per cent on his initial salary.

The government of the Province of Cordoba has approved a plan for the introduction of agricultural courses in the primary schools, presented and prepared by experts in agronomy and pedagogy, without dislocation of existing courses and schedules.

The inspectors of this Province presented for the consideration of the provincial chamber of deputies the project of a law to establish a normal school for the preparation of rural teachers exclusively, the courses offered being:

(*a*) The development of subjects related to fundamental studies in the primary schools;

(*b*) Practice teaching adapted to the needs of the primary schools of the locality; and

(*c*) Elementary teaching, both theoretical and practical, in manual arts, agriculture and cattle breeding, and minor rural industries.

Private schools conforming to governmental requirements were legally recognized and incorporated by decree of 1917 and their consequent validation effected. Pupils of the fifth and sixth grades of such private schools applying for leaving certificates are required to undergo an examination upon all subjects for those grades of the official national programs before a board of three members appointed by the inspector.

Officially apart from the Ministry of Public Education but calling for special mention was the establishment in 1917 under the encouragement of the National Department of Agriculture of 16 schools in rural domestic science in nine Provinces, including Buenos Aires. Courses are offered in minor industries, such as dairying, beekeeping, care of fowls, hog raising, agriculture, horticulture, and canning of fruits and vegetables. Five hundred women have been enrolled. A number of these schools, the largest at Tucuman, have been put on a permanent basis, and private associations are working to effect this in many places.

School celebrations of national festivals, long popular in Argentina, have been especially marked during the year 1918, the centennial year for the nation. They were held in all schools on July 8, the chief feature being the oath to the flag and the singing of the national hymn in the presence of the school and civic authorities.

Changes under the Projected Law of 1918.

Following the former order of education in Argentina, the second stage of primary education began with the educational bill submitted with the approval of the President to the Federal Congress in August, 1918. In this were incorporated changes of far wider scope than any ever before projected. Not only primary education, but the entire fabric of Argentine education was to be nationalized in content of courses, in methods of instruction, and in special preparation of teachers for tasks devolving on them under the new régime. The bill provided for large development of industrial and vocational courses and called for the use of materials peculiarly national and local. It laid stress upon civic and patriotic training, in view of the heterogeneous constitution of the Argentine population through steady streams of immigration and the necessity of molding these diverse elements into a body of patriotic and intelligent citizens. It provided for the establishment of primary schools throughout the nation under more flexible financial and administrative regulations than the old, for the segregation of specific revenues for the exclusive use of the Ministry of Public Instruction, and the consequent abolition of the old system of national subsidies to individual localities. Especially in the fight against illiteracy did the projected law embody progressive features. The National Council of Education was empowered to establish standard primary schools wherever there were as many as 20 illiterate children of school age. In the message which accompanied the recommendation of the law the President pointed out that the projected law tended to give unity and stability to the several divisions of education under the direction of the department of national instruction and adapted them to the material progress of the nation and to latter-day civilization. His identification of popular education with national progress justifies a quotation at length:

> As primary education was established by law in 1864, it contains regulations which in reality have lost their original justification; for Argentine civilization now demands urgent reforms in the matter of general instruction in order to give greater consistency and reason to the latter, and in order to make it more practical, more adaptable to the various regional needs of the Republic. It is especially urgent to carry its action to all the sections of the country not yet reached by the system in order to arrive at the real aims of a truly national education. Chief among these is to eradicate illiteracy, the most patriotic task in which we can engage and the one upon whose successful execution alone can any real national progress and enlightenment rest.
>
> The institutions of higher education have continued to develop in the direction of autonomy and within the limit determined by the law of 1885; but with the primary, they demand modifications in the course and arrangement of studies in order to abolish antiquated practices and methods and to reach the level of the great modern universities of the world.
>
> Secondary instruction, in its turn, has lacked and still

lacks a law to fix it in definite form and to define its real character in accordance with constitutional precepts and the nature of our political institutions. It has existed subject to the continual change of plans and regulations, harassed by the application of widely varying educational conceptions, in a state of continuous instability, and therefore reduced to a mere administrative mechanism without power of initiative relative to its immediate needs and without sufficient social influence to realize its true aims. To remedy these evils and to fill these gaps is one of the purposes of this law, in which the attempt has been made to include only that which ought to be general and permanent. The primary aim of secondary education should be to spread education among the towns and cities in such a way that in all the country there shall be trained, educated citizens fitted to play their part in the future civilization of the country. Preparatory instruction has therefore been kept under the control of the universities, which will fix their courses of study, their duration, and their extension both general and special. Both the plans of the preparatory courses, as well as those of the professions taught in the faculties of the university, have been projected along the lines already mentioned. The programs of the normal schools have been formulated in accordance with the technical ideas which should distinguish them, separating the general studies from those properly called pedagogical or professional, arranging them so that the former shall precede and the latter be intensified toward the end of the course.

As regards practical subjects of instruction, the project outlines only the general features according to which they must be taught. Instruction will be imparted in accordance with the necessities of the immediate field of each school, with special regard to natural production, commerce, industries, and aptitudes of the population, all with the purpose of adjusting anew the activities of the Argentine youth, which has hitherto been by preference inclined toward the more speculative studies rather than those of practical and of immediate application. It is left to the authorities of technical education to prepare plans and courses of study adapted to each class of institutions.

Enrollment in all schools has been made absolutely free, a logical consequence of compulsory education, which has as yet never been effective, but which is an indispensible condition to placing all upon the same plane of equality, a thing inherent in the principles of republican institutions.

The Government considers that the power wielded by the nation to spread primary education in the Provinces is so ample, in the form established by this projected law, that the regulations in force concerning financial subventions are without reason or justification. Once the Provinces have complied with the duty imposed upon them by the constitution in this regard up to the limit of their capacity the accompanying responsibility of the Federal Government will disappear.

The executive, knowing the great value of the teaching profession in the general concert of human activities, seeks every means to establish and dignify the career of teacher, making it a real profession surrounded by all the honors and all the public considerations which it can legitimately claim. It is therefore sought in the reform to fix proper conditions for different categories of teachers, as well as a scale of salaries, and proportional and periodic increase, thus guaranteeing the stability of the profession and assuring it an honorable and tranquil retirement. With such aims in view for the retirement of secondary teachers, the executive has believed it equitable to establish similar lines of financial aid for pensions and for increase of salaries as those offered to the teachers of primary education.

Secondary Education.

Reference has been made to the establishment of intermediate schools, at first uniform, later differentiated, substituted for the former fifth and sixth years of the primary school and intended to bridge the chasm between the primary and the secondary schools. This marked a further innovation, in that secondary education had always been left in Argentina to the Provinces, the State nationally exercising only a nominal oversight of this division. For financial reasons, as well as because of the necessity of giving uniformity to a type so widely scattered, the intermediate school was from the very first regarded as national in scope. It may be likened in many respects to the junior high school of American cities. It was designed to give instruction of a general and cultural nature in languages, history, geography, and mathematics, combined with experimental studies in the elements of physical and natural science. Much earlier entrance, its advocates claimed, would thus be possible upon subjects of vocational and technical character, which should test the nascent abilities and aptitudes of the pupil. Especial attention was to be given woodworking, typewriting, stenography, linotyping, decorative design, photography, and special arts and crafts favored by local conditions.

This experiment, though marking an advance in educational methods, was unsuccessful, and after a year of existence such schools were discontinued. They did, however, affect instruction in secondary education, leaving their impress in the radical requirement of early specialization after the fifth and sixth higher primary grades.

The educational policy of Argentina thus returned to its traditional status; and secondary education still centers around the 37 colegios nacionales, institutions for boys of 10 to 14 years of age, which admit those with leaving certificates from the fifth and sixth grades of the higher primary schools, and by revisal of 1911 offer courses arranged by fourfold division of subjects into the physical-mathematical, the chemical-biological, the historical-geographical, and the literary-philosophical groups. A decree of the National Council dated February, 1916, made the certificate of sixth grade of the public school obligatory for admission to the colegio. This was regarded as going far toward settling two fundamental difficulties—the first, the long desired abolition of the entrance examination, as discredited by experience and prejudicial to secondary training, and the second, the official recognition of the compulsory attendance law for children of 6 to 14 years.

Among the new subjects assigned for the colegios is the study of Italian, now restored after being abolished by previous decree. In accordance with this requirement, a course in this language has been instituted in the normal schools for the preparation of teachers.

The close connection of the interests of the colegio nacionale with the university is brought out in the report of the rector of the National University of Buenos Aires for 1916. It is of significance as striking out new lines in what had always been a conservative division, and carried weight in the fluid state of public opinion on education which prevailed just at that time.

Taking up the instructional aspect of secondary education, and the claims put forward by zealous partisans of the opposing views that the colegios should prepare either for higher studies or for practical life, but not for both, he urged legal provisions for both forms of training to supply the demand felt in all modern states for men of thought as well as efficiency in action. In the light of this demand all wrangling as to programs of study could only be to the damage of the State. Since the Argentine colegios half a century ago were modeled after the French lycées, with their emphasis upon the cultural studies, the world had moved far, economically and socially, and sane modifications in secondary education now clamored for recognition.

On the side of administration the peculiar question for Argentina, the land of great distances and many climates and productions, was whether the best organization for secondary instruction was the concentration of power in the hands of a council or of the minister of public instruction, or more or less complete autonomy to be granted to the individual institution. In either case the fixed principle was to be accepted that the universities were directly concerned in the discipline and studies of the students they were to receive, and that they should therefore have the right of intervening in matters of organization and studies of the colegios.

A just decentralization of the colegios could be easily realized and would bring such beneficial results as: (1) More direct and immediate action of the authorities; (2) closer articulation of the colegios with the universities in the matter of studies for preparation for the latter; (3) formation of intellectual groups that would be encouraged to take root permanently in the Provinces, thus avoiding the wholesale migration of the directing classes to the capital; (4) ease of reform, as contrasted with the present system, wherein every change in the program of studies was a disturbance whose utility was not always certain; (5) the best selection, so far as possible, of the personal directive staff of the colegios, as the men in higher education would be familiar with the problems of secondary instruction; (6) economy of administrative expense; (7) the possibility of transforming certain of the colegios into schools of arts, trades, and industries in which general instruction, continuing the primary, might be combined with the special and technical preparation so much needed for the material well-being of the several regions of the Republic.

In the projected law of public instruction, introduced in August, 1918, it is provided that all matters relating to secondary education shall be under the authority of the national universities, with full power to regulate content of courses, curricula, etc. This is manifestly a step suggested by the traditional system of Spain, in which the standard secondary schools (*institutos*) are arranged according to university districts and are governed by university rector and council. Its wisdom and advisability for a country of the Western Hemisphere have been variously considered.

Technical Education.

By the projected law of August, 1918, a National Board of Technical Education is to be established to ascertain the progress of this branch of education in other countries, to adapt whatever may be possible to the conditions and needs of Argentina, to foster technical instruction in the national schools, and to keep in touch with its progress throughout the world.

Normal-School Training.

The sequence of studies prescribed for pupils of the normal school according to the decree of March, 1916, is also worthy of notice. Immediately following, and based upon the intermediate schools which, as described above, were discarded after trial, the normal school required four years for the teachers' diploma, after which the student might proceed to higher studies for the degree of teacher of modern languages in two years or that of teacher of languages in normal school in three years, or that of teacher of philosophy in any institution in six years. A commendable gain of one year in each of these was effected, and this feature is to be embodied in the new provisions now under consideration. In addition, the new project of educational law outlines a teacher's course of four years, clearly differentiating between the general or cultural and the pedagogical or professional courses. The former are assigned to the first three years as required; the latter are reserved for the last year, constituting an intensive curriculum of pedagogical history and methods and practice teaching in the required annexed practice school. The completion (1918) of the Normal School Sarmiento in Buenos Aires, named in honor of the founder of popular education in South America, is to be noted. This school, capable of accommodating 1,000 pupils and equipped with the most modern apparatus, is worthy of comparison with the finest schools in the other countries educationally most advanced.

Higher Education.

With the provision incorporated in the projected law, by which control of national secondary education is vested in the universities, the latter will touch national education much more intimately than ever before. The universities of Argentina are those of Buenos Aires, Cordoba, and La Plata, which are national, and those of Santa Fe and Tucuman, which are provincial but will soon be nationalized. In 1917 there was a growing feeling in university circles in favor of decentralization, with greater degree of autonomy for each university. The report of the rector of the university of Buenos Aires for 1917 was of interest as showing the effect of this upon the colegios as well as the universities. How far this has been checked by the projected provision to intrust secondary education to universities can not be learned.

The unrest among the student bodies in the institutions of higher education has constituted perhaps the most remarkable feature of the educational history of the past year. In Buenos Aires reform was demanded in the statutes under which the university was governed, and the adoption of methods in conformity with new tendencies in university instruction. The students demanded especially the right to vote for the election of the authorities. Satisfactory agreement was reached, and the university, after several days of suspension of classes and demonstrations on the part of the student body, resumed instruction, which was uninterrupted for the rest of the year. At the University of Cordoba the conflict between the students and the authorities assumed more serious proportions. Regular work was suspended, the efforts of the mediator appointed by the National Government to hear the claims of the student body and to decide upon the just and practical course for the university authorities to adopt were unsatisfactory to the complainants, and the authority of the minister of public instruction was invoked. Upon investigation the latter official advocated in his report to the executive a complete reorganization of the university in its statutes, regulations, acts of discipline, and staff of professors. These changes were ratified by the executive and were practically embodied in the project of the law submitted to the Congress in those sections pertaining to university education. In the other three universities, those of La Plata, Tucuman, and Santa Fe, the disturbances which impeded the prosecution of the regular routine of studies were comparatively insignificant, though the spirit of unrest was marked and many of the reforms and changes secured in the two leading universities were readily accepted.

The growth of the so-called student centers (*centros estudiantiles*) has been a feature of higher education during the past two years. These organizations have come to be representative of student life and of the student point of view, and have therefore gained much importance in the eyes of the authorities. They are organized according to departments of studies, such as the centers of medical and dental students, of engineering students, of political science students, of students of architecture, and of law. Each numbers from 100 to 500 members. They are grouped as a whole into the University Federation of Buenos Aires, in which each is represented by delegates, and which is regarded as the mouthpiece of all university students in the metropolis.

Plans are already under way by the executive council of the University of Buenos Aires for the celebration of the first centenary of its foundation, which will occur in October, 1921. Invitations have been extended to the institutions of higher education in all countries of the world to designate and send representatives. Though the actual building of the ancient colegio nacional, in which the university began its operation, has been materially changed, yet the present building occupies the same site, and it has been decided to hold the centennial celebration in it.

Of interest is the projected foundation of a popular university at Buenos Aires, constituted along industrial lines and frankly designed to counteract the technical and industrial influence of North American universities in South American countries.

A survey of educational progress in Argentina may fittingly conclude with mention of the annual American Congress of Education and Commercial Extension, held in Montevideo in January, 1919, in which representatives of all the Latin-American countries participated, and those of Argentina, from her economic and educational leadership, were most prominent. The proceedings of the congress will be discussed in the chapter on Uruguay.

Vocational Education in Brazil.

Educational activity in Brazil has been most marked in the field of vocational education. A special commission, appointed by the Director General of Public Instruction, consisting of five experienced teachers in subjects of this nature, was instructed to formulate courses for the State schools which were to be established by law in the Federal District. They were to serve as models for subsequent schools of the same character in the several States and Territories. The commission, of which Senhor Coryntho da Fonseca was the spokesman, after several months of conference and personal visits of inspection to the vocational schools already existent in the several centers, especially in Sao Paulo, and after hearing reports from active teachers in the subjects, presented its report in March, 1919. It was approved by the Vice President, serving ad interim for the President, and was recommended by him to be put into actual operation pending its formal enactment into law by the Congress.

The report as finally presented rested upon four main considerations:

1. The State, in the field of instruction, has primarily an educational function and only secondarily a vocational one. Courses in shop training, designed to awake and develop an aptitude in the pupil for a particular industry, must of course enter into any well-rounded scheme of education. This in turn must be designed to promote a general and not a specialized technical education which will introduce both sexes to industrial and commercial life. For practical reasons of expense, if for no other, the State should not be expected to prepare pupils for specialized vocations.

2. The task of the commission being to deal with the branches of vocational training best adapted to give the pupil a broad outlook upon

general industrial activities, the commission judged it best to confine its recommendations to manual work of construction in wood, metal, and plastic material. In methods as well as content of instruction it is emphasized that such work must proceed along the lines of teaching by example. In such teaching much that is old and fundamental must be stressed by way of throwing light upon the elements of the training that are common to all branches of manual arts.

3. In its decision to urge a general attitude toward industrial training rather than specialized methods peculiar to one branch, the commission was confirmed by the testimony of all except one of the directors of the vocational institutions in Brazil. Only one advocated specialized instruction. Written representations of the faculties of the vocational schools Alvaro Baptista, and Souza Aguiar, in Rio, further confirmed this view.

4. The results of vocational instruction in Brazil as actually observed within the last few years convinced the commission—

(*a*) That unspecialized training best provided the foundations for good citizenship as well as industrial training.

(*b*) That by this training the latent technical aptitudes of the student were more effectively revealed and developed, as shown by steady increase in salaries of the graduates, than was the case with the apprentices who had been trained exclusively in one line.

(*c*) That the superior adaptation of the graduates of the general vocational school had been shown by tables giving information as to their progress in skill and value to their employers. These tables were naturally incomplete, but their general drift was undeniable.

(*d*) That the chief cause of the poor attendance upon the vocational instruction for boys is the prevalent idea that the vocational school is an index of lower social standing, enrolling only those boys that can not obtain any other means of education. Thus the vocational school is sharply differentiated socially from other types of schools. It suffers from being regarded as preeminently the school to train workmen. The commission had in mind the purpose of preparing public sentiment for the passing of this traditional prejudice when it attempted to inspire a just estimate of manual work in the public mind and to organize such courses as would adequately carry out this idea.

(*e*) That the vocational school must be established as a direct continuation of the primary school, ministering to the innate tendency in the child to realize things with his own hands; that thus the traditional and depressing prejudice mentioned would be counteracted, as time would not be given for it to intervene in the child's mind. The workshop, thus articulated with general training, would come to be the fulfillment of an aspiration, inculcating as well the love of work and respect for it.

(*f*) That the success of the projected schools depends largely upon the cooperation of the industrial firms of Brazil, which should be appealed to for their sympathy and for the encouragement of their adolescent employees to attend these schools; that the granting of daylight hours to employees to attend such schools, as has been done in England and France, with the consequent improvement in the physical and mental condition of the pupils, is a step to be commended to all employers as patriotic citizens.

The salient provisions of the report of the commission are as follows:

> ARTICLE 1. The technical and vocational instruction maintained by the prefecture of the Federal District has for its aim to complete the primary elementary instruction by means of a general technical education leading the youth of both sexes preferably to industrial and commercial activities.
>
> ART. 2. Technical and vocational instruction shall be given in the following types of schools:
>
> (*a*) Primary vocational schools.
>
> (*b*) Secondary vocational institutes.
>
> (*c*) Secondary agricultural schools.
>
> (*d*) Vocational finishing courses.
>
> (*e*) Normal school of arts and crafts.

Types (*a*), (*d*), and (*e*) shall be day schools exclusively; types (*b*) and (*c*) shall offer boarding accommodations for pupils from distance.

ART. 3. In schools of types (*a*) and (*d*) instruction shall be imparted predominantly in the recitation rooms.

ART. 4. The courses of the primary vocational school for boys shall include the following subjects:

(*a*) The usual subjects of the complementary course of the primary schools, with fuller development of the studies of physics, chemistry, natural history, hygiene, and mathematics.

(*b*) Modeling and free-hand and mechanical drawing.

ART. 5. The courses of the primary vocational school for girls shall include:

(*a*) The usual subjects of the complementary course of the primary schools, with fuller development of the studies of hygiene and domestic economy.

(*b*) Modeling and free-hand drawing.

ART. 6. The subjects of the vocational finishing courses shall include:

(*a*) In the commercial course, Portuguese and civic instruction, commercial geography, French and one other modern language, English or German, to be chosen by the pupil, commercial correspondence and accounting, typewriting, stenography, and arithmetic.

(*b*) In the industrial course, Portuguese and civic instruction, arithmetic, and geography, elements of applied physics, chemistry, and natural history, accounting as related to the particular vocation selected by the pupil, free-hand and mechanical drawing.

ART. 7. The vocational finishing courses are designed primarily for young men already employed in industry and commerce, who seek to improve their vocational knowledge.

ART. 8. The two types of vocational finishing schools may be taught conjointly in the same building.

ART. 9. Teachers and assistants imparting instruction shall be appointed as follows:

(*a*) There shall be a teacher and so many assistants for each branch as shall be made necessary by the attendance.

(*b*) For the instruction in technical accounting related to each vocation there shall be employed special teachers only where 15 or more students are enrolled for each course, and they shall receive salaries only when actually teaching. The same teachers shall be in charge of the various related branches of technical instruction in the shops.

ART. 10. The courses in the secondary vocational institutes for boys shall include—

(*a*) The elementary and middle instruction for pupils who have not had them.

(*b*) Physical exercises and military drill.

(*c*) Vocal and instrumental music.

ART. 11. The courses in the vocational institutes for girls shall include—

(*a*) Primary instruction for such pupils as have not had it.

(*b*) Vocational drawing and modeling.

In the vocational institutes the elementary primary instruction shall be followed by an intensive course in manual arts, such as sloyd, wood carving, and weaving in straw, vine, and bamboo.

Art. 12. The primary vocational schools shall also offer a commercial course consisting of the following subjects:

(*a*) Commercial correspondence and accounting.

(*b*) Typewriting and stenography.

(*c*) French and one other modern language, English or German.

Art. 13. Instruction in the workshops of vocational schools for boys shall be given first in a general compulsory course of three years, during which the pupil shall in turn be trained in the workshops in cold and molten metals, including foundry work and wrought-iron work. The pupil shall then be allowed to specialize in any workshop or section at his choice. The pupils of the vocational institutes for boys shall likewise take a compulsory course in horticulture and kindred subjects.

Art. 14. The agricultural schools and the vocational institutes shall require attendance on the courses of civil training and agronomy, with optional specialization in any line selected when the general course is completed.

Art. 15. In the vocational schools and institutes for girls there shall be a compulsory general course upon the following practical subjects: Cooking, laundering, ironing and starching, housekeeping, sewing and dressmaking. Along with this general course the pupils shall attend certain vocational courses chosen by themselves from sewing, lace making, and embroidery, artificial-flower work, etc.

Art. 16. For admission to the schools of vocational instruction the following shall be the legal requirements as to age:

(*a*) For vocational and agricultural schools, minimum age 13, maximum 21.

(*b*) For the vocational institutes for boys, minimum age 10, maximum 13.

(*c*) For the vocational institutes for girls, minimum age 7, maximum 13.

(*d*) For the normal school of arts and trades, minimum age 14, maximum 25.

(*e*) For the vocational finishing courses, minimum age 13.

ART. 17. For matriculation in the vocational and agricultural schools and the finishing courses the candidates shall submit to an examination upon the subjects taught in the middle course of the primary school. In the commercial courses of the finishing schools, in the girls' schools, and in the normal school of arts and trades, the entrance examination shall be upon the subjects of the final examination of the primary schools.

ART. 18. The school year in the entire system of vocational instruction, with the exception of agricultural schools, shall begin March 1 and close November 30. The period from December 1 to December 24 shall be devoted to examinations and to school exhibitions. In the agricultural schools, because of their nature, the pupils shall have 60 days of annual vacation granted to them in groups by the director in accordance with the demands of the agricultural seasons and labors.

ART. 19. The courses of the primary vocational schools, of the institutes, and of the finishing courses shall be divided into periods of 4 to 5 years; the finishing courses into periods of three years; and the commercial course of the schools for girls into a period of two years.

Art. 24. The officials of inspection of technical and vocational instruction shall draw up annual statistics of attendance and of the results of the vocational instruction upon the bases of data furnished by the directors of the several schools and, so far as possible, by employers and by the former pupils who have themselves left the schools. These statistics shall relate to the following topics:

(*a*) Number of pupils placed, with indication of the establishments where they are employed.

(*b*) Initial salary obtained by them as related to the period of schooling.

(*c*) Technical aptitude revealed by former pupils and their capacity of adaptation to the various industrial works.

(*d*) Progress of increase in salary of former pupils.

(*e*) All available information as to individual former pupils with regard to the advantages or disadvantages of their schooling in the decision of economic life, and their success in it.

Art. 25. All posts of assistants and substitutes in the vocational system shall be filled by competitive examinations.

(*a*) For the assistant in drawing in the vocational schools in institutes for boys, the examination shall be tests in drawing, in artistic training, and in pedagogical fitness.

(*b*) For the filling of the same post in the vocational schools and institutes for girls the examination shall be tests in writing at dictation, in decorative composition, in embroidery and lacework, and in pedagogical fitness.

(*c*) The competitive test for filling the post of substitutes in shopwork shall be upon vocational design of an assigned theme for shopwork and the execution of the same.

ART. 26. The teachers in vocational instruction shall be named by means of promotion of the assistants and substitutes.

ART. 27. There shall be a substitute for every group of 20 pupils in shopwork, and an assistant for every class of 30 pupils.

ART. 28. When any primary school is transformed into a vocational school there shall be annexed the elementary primary course in which shall be taught intensively the manual arts prescribed for the elementary instruction of the institutes, but the pupils shall attend the shopwork of the vocational courses only when they have completed the work of the middle course and attained the age of 13 years.

Education in Chile.

Preliminary.

The last two years have seen in Chile a distinct gathering up of the threads of educational purpose. The feeling of dissatisfaction with the primary school system, for many years inarticulate, has found a voice, and all signs point to Chile's finally securing a modernized system of public instruction. The head and front of the indictment drawn by national students of education has been the complete Germanization of the system through the employment of a considerable number of German educational experts during the decade from 1904 to 1914. The climax came in the revelations of the propagandist activities of the German educators brought out at the meeting of the National Educational Association in 1917.

Financial support of public instruction in Chile has never been stinted, so far as its existent state was concerned. As merely one item may be adduced the fact that in March, 1916, the Congress authorized the President to devote to public instruction for specific aims such as the building and remodeling of schoolhouses, $4,000,000 annually for 10 years, through the medium of the Central Council of Education, in which was vested the discretion as to methods and objects of the expenditure. In 1918 the budget was voted by the Congress of $35,450,000 for public instruction, as against that of $32,373,404 for 1917. So that the authorities of the Government must justly be credited with a practical interest in education which encourages teachers and other active workers in their efforts toward greater efficiency.

In 1917 there had been increased discussion of matters educational; and in June of that year President Sanfuentes in his message showed that the time had come to impress on the national system of public instruction a more practical stamp, making it adequate to the needs of everyday life and the special conditions of the country. Along with this he urged the specialization of secondary education as, just then, the urgent and opportune point of attack for the development of Chile's scientific and industrial possibilities.

This message was followed by action of the Congress which clearly showed the traditional line of cleavage long prevailing in Chile's social and political system. The demand for some form of modernized public instruction could no longer be repressed; and a conservative deputy introduced the project of a law to insert in the constitution a provision for compulsory primary schooling and compulsory religious instruction, the only modification of the latter being the concession to the parent to choose the forms and means of such instruction. The radical party was not slow in countering with a project adopting the feature of compulsory attendance but decentralizing and completely secularizing the existing system. The latter proposal, now made for the first time in the history of Chilean legislation, was especially bold, as Chile has never done away with the essentially religious tone of her education. She retains representatives of the State church on her National Council of Education, freely recognizes parochial primary schools, and has her secondary schools largely managed by religious instructors and under distinctively religious auspices.

The compromise bill formulated by a specially appointed commission of the Congress sought to satisfy both extremes. It vested supreme administrative authority in educational matters in a council of 18, sitting in Santiago, presided over by the Minister of Justice and Instruction; but it allowed 11 of the members to be named by the Senate, the Chamber of Deputies, and the President of the Republic. This feature was severely criticized by the liberals and by the National Educational Association as still keeping educational authority in the hands of politicians, not intrusting it to men really interested in education, and making it possible to block all educational progress whenever desired.

The bill made four years' attendance in primary schools, private or public, compulsory for all children between 7 and 13, and required all reaching the latter age without completing the prescribed course to continue until 15. Poverty could not be pleaded in excuse, as grants by the State were specified and graduated in amounts according to need. Exemption from religious instruction was allowed upon written application of the parent or upon certification of the local junta, another feature opposed by the National Educational Association on the ground that the junta's powers could never be so amplified legally. Programs of study and schedules should be under the authority of the inspector general of primary instruction. Primary instruction was to be imparted to complete illiterates in schools called supplementary, managed independently of existing primary schools, and to partial illiterates in schools called complementary, conducted in conjunction with existent primary schools.

The bill, as outlined above, encountered opposition from many sources, and still remains unenacted. Pending its passage, the Minister of Public Instruction, by virtue of the power vested in him, issued in 1918 a decree organizing primary education in three grades of two years each, continued by one grade of vocational education of from one to three years. Attendance is not specifically compulsory, though the local junta has power so to declare it in the schools of its jurisdiction. The requirements as to qualifications of a primary teacher are made more rigorous; he must be a citizen of Chile, of good character, not less than 18 nor more than 40 years of age at the time of appointment, and a graduate of a Government normal school, or holding a degree of a Chilean or recognized foreign institution.

Illiteracy.

The problem of illiteracy in Chile is a serious one, the estimated figures for 1917 showing 959,061 illiterates out of a total population of 3,249,279. Since the year 1900 the struggle against it has grown in vigor. The National Educational Association has shown especial efficiency, and has worked through committees having the following phases in charge: Compulsory school attendance, the legal requirements, condition of the schools and the teaching force, school revenues, school buildings and sanitation, and special education.

This steady pressure prepared public sentiment for the leadership of the most influential agency ever invoked in the fight against illiteracy, viz. the conferences organized by the powerful newspaper El Mercurio. Under its auspices these conferences were held in a 3-days' series in July, 1917, and were attended and participated in by men and women identified with every phase of national education. The following topics were the salient ones of those discussed:

1. Comparative study of illiteracy statistics in various countries.
2. Means of combating illiteracy in leading nations.
3. Practicable means of action in Chile.
4. Means of contribution, and proportion in which the State, the municipal authorities, and the Provinces may contribute to the budget necessary.
5. Cooperation of private initiative.
6. Means of making school attendance compulsory.
7. Regulation of child labor.
8. Reforms necessary in actual plans of study and in classification of schools.
9. Necessity and practical means of giving the schools a more Nationalistic character.
10. Minimum of knowledge to be required by compulsory attendance law.
11. Place of night schools, Sunday schools, and traveling schools, in the struggle against illiteracy.

While no action of a legal character resulted from these conferences, yet the impetus given to the cause was powerful, and had weight in bringing about the decree and the projected law already outlined. Such a move, combining at once social and economic as well as educational characteristics, seeking to bring public opinion to bear on the solution of a problem underlying the life of a nation, and launched by a newspaper, is unique in the history of education.

The Territory of Magellanes has shown itself remarkably efficient in handling the problem of illiteracy. It is the southernmost area of the country, and little favored by nature, being a long strip of barren and rocky coast, with a climate singularly bleak and uninviting. Its industries are based exclusively upon its mineral resources; and its population, though intelligent, is very sparse. By the census of 1917, its percentage of illiteracy was 20; according to the estimate of the author of a study of the Territory, published in the Anales de la Universidad, April, 1918, this has been reduced to 7 per cent. Credit is largely due the Society of Popular Instruction, a private organization, established in 1911, which offers free instruction to pupils of all ages. In spite of the prevailing inclemency of the climate, the sessions of its day and night schools are excellently attended. The system is centralized in Punta Arenas.

Primary Education.

Unlike Argentina and Brazil, primary public education has always been left in the hands of the central national government, the individual Province having control of financial outlay and the construction of school buildings, and this only when requirements of the national law are fulfilled. Uniform programs of study and schedules of hours are enforced throughout the nation. But conditions of scarcity of materials and labor render it impossible to keep many of the old buildings in repair. The tendency long criticized by the Association of Teachers, to cram school buildings into the half dozen larger centers, seems in a fair way to be checked.[1]

This new order of things is most plainly seen in the attention paid to rural schools, which have predominated in the number built since 1916. The Government has instructed the committee on public works and the department of primary instruction to develop a plan of building uniform types of rural school. The expenses are to be borne out of the fund just mentioned. Three types are contemplated, with a capacity of 80, 160, and 400 pupils respectively, solidly constructed, conforming strictly to all modern demands of sanitation, lighting, and heating. In many places the

[1] Criticism has been freely expressed in the public press of the use of a disproportionately large part of the primary school fund voted by the Congress for the use of the executive.

North American principle of consolidation of schools has been applied, to the distinct improvement of attendance and instruction, 200 small and struggling schools having been abolished and 100 annexed to others more centrally situated. With these gains, however, the crying need in Chile is acknowledged to be more schools. It is estimated that 10,000 elementary schools are yet needed for her approximately 750,000 children, of whom slightly less than 400,000 are in the schools of this grade, and 50,000 in private parochial schools. All educational thinkers are agreed that the situation calls for legal compulsory attendance on primary instruction, rigidly enforced.

Secondary Education.

Secondary education in Chile is organized in three grades: (1) National high schools; (2) liceos of the second class, and (3) complete liceos of the first class.

(1) The high schools are a development of the last few years, and are situated only in the larger centers. They number 30 for boys and 12 for girls, enrolling less than 12,000 pupils, and are generally little more than higher elementary schools. They are almost exclusively technical, and do not prepare the pupil for advanced study.

(2) The liceos of the second class (sometimes called colegios), of which about 100 exist in the Provinces and Territories, offer courses covering three years in the elementary subjects of instruction common to scientific and literary groups.

(3) The liceos of the first class, numbering 40 for boys and 31 for girls, and offering the full course of six years, are representative of the best in secondary education in Latin-America. Those for boys, following the tradition of the Spanish system for corresponding schools, are administered by the University of Chile; those for girls, by the Minister of Public Instruction and the National Council. The practical and scientific wave which swept over this division of education in 1915 caused the reinforcement of physical and chemical teaching. Spanish, history and geography, religion (optional), French, mathematics, natural sciences, gymnastics and singing, and manual

training run through all six years of the course; English (or German or Italian), philosophy, civics, penmanship and drawing, mechanical drawing (optional), extend through varying numbers of years. Students of secondary education are struck with the excessive number of hours required weekly, the minimum being 29 for the first year and the maximum 33 for each of the last three years.

The essential purpose of the liceo of the first class is to prepare for the university, or for the professions; and national scholarships are granted, including maintenance at the hostels, or annexed boarding halls which were established five years ago.

The system of secondary education has long been criticized by Chilean educational thinkers as being too largely mental and literary, and as paying little, if any, attention to the physical and moral. The attempt to organize sports and physical exercises in secondary education has met far less encouragement than in other South American countries.

By decree of May, 1917, classes for illiterate girls over 7 years old were annexed to liceos for girls, the ministry basing the number to be admitted upon the attendance of the year previous. This was stoutly opposed by the National Educational Association as being a confusion of classification, a violation of the continuity of the educational system, and an evasion of the palpable duty of the school authorities, which should press the Government to establish fitting and proper schools for such illiterate girls.

The Government has appointed a commission of prominent men for the study of reforms necessary and advisable for programs of secondary education for girls. As matters stand, the same programs of study are set for both boys and girls, a traditional arrangement the disadvantages of which are coming fully to be recognized.

Despite unfavorable and antiquated programs of studies, the Province of Nuble has made noteworthy progress in female secondary education. In Chillan, its capital, are conducted four liceos, three of which are for girls. Ambitious courses in the classics, social sciences, and rudimentary science are offered. One of them, the Instituto Pedagogico, founded in 1912, exercises far-reaching influence over the social, moral, and artistic conditions of the Province. The American Liceo, a private institution, conducted by teachers from the United States, devotes especial attention to the teaching of English, colloquial and literary, and also gives instruction generally along thoroughly modern high-school lines.

Training of Teachers.

Chile's system of training teachers is distinctively eclectic, borrowing, as it has done, from France, Sweden, Germany, and the United States. Before 1870 French influence predominated, the great Argentine educator, Sarmiento, himself a pupil of the school of Saint-Simon, having founded the first normal school in 1842 while in exile from the tyranny of the dictator Rosas. German influence became pronounced about 1880, when that nation began to supply men and women teachers in the normals and as instructors in all grades of education. Since 25 years ago the tide began to turn toward North American influence, especially of the type of education developed in the Northwestern States. The Chilean ideal is a judicious combination of (1) an institution for the training of teachers for public schools who shall have adequate culture, specialized training, manual skill, and theoretical and practical knowledge of modern subjects, and (2) an institution for training in social relations and habits, exercising steady influence on the social environment of the school by means of popular courses and conferences, and participation in popular movements.

The full course in the 16 training colleges for teachers covers five years, of which the first three are devoted to general education and the last two to professional training. The course for the fifth year is essentially professional, consisting of pedagogy (history, methodology, and practice teaching), 17 hours weekly; Spanish, 1 hour; English or French or German, 4 hours; civics and economics, 2 hours; hygiene, 2 hours; horticulture or metallography, 2 hours; drawing, 1 hour; manual arts, 2 hours; music, 1 hour; physical education, 3 hours. All expenses are defrayed, in return for which the pupil is pledged to teach for seven years in the national schools.

The actual method of instruction is along German lines. Object lessons, those in natural history and history and geography have all impressed recent foreign visitors as essentially Herbartian. Perhaps in no other country of the world, since the well-drilled German schools fell into chaos, is the influence of the normal schools upon the system and method of public instruction more powerful than in Chile. Indeed, this potent influence has overleaped the boundaries of Chile proper and affected every country of Latin America. A supreme example is the influence of the Instituto Pedagogico, the best known of Chilean normal schools, founded in 1909, with predominatingly German faculty, which has developed into a type of higher normal school with a colegio annexed, emphasizing practice teaching with subsequent criticism and courses of general pedagogy and methodology in every subject. Its certificates rank highest in the secondary and normal education of the capital city; students are attracted to it from the other Latin-American States, and return home to reorganize education there along its lines. Its boast is that it inspired the establishment of the Instituto Nacional at Buenos Aires.

Scandinavian and Belgian influences are at work in the Instituto de Profesores Especiales. Established in 1906, it was definitely reorganized in 1910 and installed in the building especially constructed for it. Of its 300 pupils 200 are women, and the majority of both men and women are active teachers in the schools of the capital. It offers courses common to all the specialized sections, such as psychology, French, pedagogy, civics, and school legislation, and includes five sections, fundamental to its organization: Physical education, manual arts, drawing and penmanship, domestic economy, and vocal music. For the convenience of teachers, instruction is given from 7 to 9 a.m. and from 4 to 8 p.m.

The last few years have seen wide extension of the demand for rural normal schools, and many critics of the existent schools have urged that they follow those of the State of Wisconsin as a model. The essential solidarity of educational aims of the South American republics is shown by the fact that Chile, Argentina, and Bolivia during the same period drew their inspiration from the same North American source.

The decree already mentioned under the head of primary education emphasizes the duty of the normal schools to prepare free of all expense primary teachers for any of the three grades of instruction. Each normal school is also required to have annexed such specially organized practice schools as shall be necessary. At the discretion of the President of the Republic, the normal schools shall offer special courses for those students who have passed the examinations of the fifth year of the colegios, with the aim of attracting such students into the field of teaching. That the need of wider training of the teachers is a pressing one in Chile is shown by the fact that, in 1915, of 3,000 rural teachers, only 350, and of 6,240 primary teachers of the nation at large, only 2,435, had normal school training. The service had to be recruited by 2,000 graduates of primary schools who passed examinations, and by 1,850 applicants who held no certificate and were allowed to serve as temporary substitutes.

Of special interest is the annual reciprocity of teachers between the Government of Chile and the Universities of the States of California and Washington, arranged in 1918. Each party is to send four. For the present the Chilean commission has expressed predominant interest in secondary education, and has called for one university professor, one normal-school teacher, one teacher of technical subjects, and one teacher (preferably a woman) in secondary education. The universities mentioned will act as the agents in the selection of the instructors.

Interchange of university professors has also been arranged with Uruguay, which is for the present confined to medical instruction.

The National Educational Association has at many meetings pressed for the scientific and practical training of the teachers of Chile in vocational studies; and for the appropriation by the Congress of a definite sum for sending normal teachers abroad for study in the modern practical and sociological subjects.

Technical Education.

For this branch of education the National Educational Association in 1917 recommended that there be established by law a Council of Industrial Education composed of a director and 12 members, four of whom shall be professors of the fundamental technical branches, one a woman inspector of vocational schools for women, one an inspector general of primary education, one the director general of railroads, and one a director and inspector of army munitions. Their duties should be to exercise superintendency over the entire system of technical and industrial education to be organized in the Republic, over the national school of arts and trades, and over such industrial schools for girls and women as might be established. On this board should be likewise all inspectors and officials of such branches as might be later established. A bill embodying these provisions was introduced in the Congress but has not as yet been acted upon.

Steady progress in all branches of technical education has been shown. The schools of higher primary grade offering technical courses number 288, with physical training and gymnastics compulsory in all grades. There were also in operation 29 technical colegios for women; 6 agricultural colegios; 10 commercial schools, controlled by the commission upon commercial education; and 3 schools of mines.

The department of industrial promotion has urged upon the Congress the establishment of a chain of industrial and agricultural schools.

With the establishment by law of the Industrial University of Valparaiso there will be completed the full cycle of industrial education in Chile, consisting of: (1) Elementary industrial training in two schools already established and in six more to be established; (2) secondary industrial training in the School of Arts and Crafts; and (3) higher industrial training in the Technical School of Valparaiso.

In November, 1918, met the first National Congress of Dairying, organized under the auspices of the Agronomic Society of Chile. It urged the legal organization of instruction in this branch in (1) special schools of dairying in northern and central Chile; (2) courses annexed to already established schools of agriculture; (3) in establishments of secondary education for youths of both sexes in popular meetings and public traveling courses; (4) in rural primary schools for illiterate adults.

It is appropriate to mention just here the comprehensive project of the board of missions of the Methodist Episcopal Church of the United States for the establishment of an agricultural and industrial system of education in southern Chile. It has been approved by the Government of Chile as a potent aid in the uplift of the peon class. A ranch of nearly 4,000 acres has been purchased along the Malleco River, on which it is purposed to train the native population in the rudimentary subjects of instruction, and especially in modern agricultural methods. The management will employ the best available experts in horticulture, agriculture, and domestic arts to be found in the South American countries who may be acquainted with the needs of Chilean rural life.

The National Educational Association of Chile.

This body plays a larger part in educational thought and leadership than the corresponding body in any other Latin American State. Its activities are planned for close articulation of the social and educational needs of the nation. One of the furthest reaching is the public-extension work in subjects of university and secondary instruction. In 1917, its eleventh year of operation, it held 14 conferences at the University of Chile, with an attendance of 15,000, an increase of 50 per cent over the previous year. The subjects treated were patriotic, historical, literary, artistic, sociological, commercial, and medico-therapeutic.

In secondary extension during 1917 there were held in provincial capitals 19 conferences on subjects more popular and more exclusively educational and sociological.

The department of university extension has also for three years devoted itself to collecting international data upon immigration and naturalization laws, and has cooperated with all the labor organizations of the Republic to hinder the passage of premature and unscientific laws in this field.

The activities of the association cover a wide range. In his report for the year 1917 the president reviewed the activities of the body and examined the most important problems to which it had addressed itself during the period. They were:

1. The establishment of a rural normal school, a project not yet realized.

2. Democratic education by the progressive elimination of primary courses of education in secondary institutions.

3. Obligatory primary instruction, sought by a law passed by the Chamber of Deputies in 1917, but as yet not acted upon by the Senate.

4. Nationalization of the Chilean system of education, a question which needs to be presented still more in detail to the nation and the Congress.

Like Argentina, Chile has a grave problem in the assimilation of alien elements, and her nationalism is alarmed at the activity of the school organizations of diverse races existent on her soil. French students of education are intensely interested in this development as a vindication of their prophecies, for they have long been pointing out the Germanization of Chilean education.

The association has vigorously urged legislation requiring the close and systematic inspection of all nongovernmental schools, especially those of secondary grade in north Chile, where German propaganda has for years been an open secret, carried on, as was well known, by a German-Chilean Union of Teachers, and where German liceos exist in full operation. The association urged the requirement in secondary schools of essentially national subjects, such as Spanish and the history, geography, and civics of Chile, taught by Chileans and descendants of Chileans.

In the field of physical education, the activities of the association have been specially directed to securing proper playgrounds for schools and to arousing practical interest in this field among philanthropists and the public at large. The association has taken strong ground for antialcoholic instruction in primary and secondary schools, urging that such be incorporated in the textbooks in the study of physiology, hygiene, and temperance, and in independent courses in public schools and State colegios. The project encountered opposition in the National Congress. The association has also grappled with the problem of immorality, issuing in May, 1917, appeals to families on sexual ethics and the systematic inculcation of ethical ideas of sex by educational and therapeutic measures. During 1917, fraternal relations were established with Brazil and Bolivia, on the occasion of the inauguration of the Higher Normal Institute.

Education in Uruguay.

General Introduction.

The marked educational awakening of Uruguay during the last biennium has been only one phase of the universal demand of the nation for a new social and economic adjustment. Perhaps the chief manifestation of this has been the adoption of the new constitution in place of the old, which had been in force exactly 90 years. At a plebiscite of November, 1917, the constitution as formulated was submitted to the people and adopted by a vote of 85,000 to 4,000; and it became the fundamental law of the land on March 1, 1919. As regards its bearings upon educational administration, the most noteworthy change—and perhaps that around which centered most opposition during its consideration—was the provision which divides the executive power between a President and a National Council of Administration.

The latter body, composed of nine members elected for six years directly by the people, and absolutely independent of the President, has charge of all matters relating to public instruction, public works, labor, industries, public charities, health, and the preparation of the annual national budget. The administrative officers of public instruction of all grades, including the minister, are appointed by the National Council and are subject to its authority according to such particular laws and regulations as the Congress may enact. This substitution of a composite board for an individual as the fountainhead of educational authority is an experiment whose operations will be observed with much interest in a country of South America habituated by tradition to authority concentrated in an individual.

Illiteracy.

Instruction of adults and the night schools.—The problem of combating illiteracy, as in all the more progressive South American countries during the last biennium, has received more systematic consideration than during any previous period.[2] As will be seen later in the consideration of the rural schools, measures have been taken which are of unusual importance for the instruction of youthful illiterates. In the related field of instruction of adults who are illiterates or nearly so, work of a creative nature has been done in Uruguay. The mere statistics show progress, the courses offered for adults in the year 1916-17 being 55 in excess of the former year and the enrollment 5,284, an increase of 1,671 over that year; but the new spirit animating this branch is the notable feature. The authorities have kept it steadily in mind to carry adult education out from the capital city to the rural districts; and the national authorities of primary education have cooperated efficiently in lending schoolhouses as places for adult instruction and encouraging primary teachers to assist in this work. The Government has furthered the study of the problem in the researches of Señor Hipolito Coirolo, director of the largest night school for adults in Montevideo. Señor Coirolo spent nearly two years in collecting systematic data from Argentina, Brazil, Colombia, and Paraguay, which were naturally confronted by the same problems in adult illiteracy. In March, 1917, he presented to the authorities the results of his findings in a project for the organic reform of instruction for adults in the night schools. Señor Coirolo maintained that the time was ripe for progress in this field to keep pace with the other educational demands, more especially as it was admitted that the prevailing system was a more or less poorly made combination of regulations and practices covering many localities and periods, and had been only tentatively adopted by presidential decree in 1903, and given legal existence in 1907, when 35 night schools were organized. All familiar with conditions knew that they were now completely out of touch with modern social and educational demands.

Señor Coirolo found the curriculum of night schools too largely theoretical and bookish and in only a few instances offering practical instruction. After careful study of the subjects offered in the night schools of progressive countries, he urged that the night schools of the future be

[2] See executive message of May, 1917, accompanying project of law for appropriation of $50,000 for appointment of 100 assistant primary teachers for the Departments of the Republic.

organized upon the following main lines:

1. The completion of 17 years of age requisite for admission.

2. The division into three classes, each occupying a year according to the degree of illiteracy, and the division of each class into three cycles of three months each, the cycle to be the unit of time, without limitation upon the transfer of pupils from one cycle to another.

3. The subjects to be introduced in logical sequence and to be taught in accordance with the development of the pupil and to consist of reading, language work, writing, arithmetic, elements of applied geometry, singing, drawing, moral instruction, elements of anatomy, physiology, hygiene, civic instruction, geography, and history (national and universal); talks and lessons on objects of daily life, manual arts, domestic economy, and household arts; elements of political economy, sociology, psychology, duties of parents, accounting, and industrial training. Individual conferences with teachers, reading, writing, and arithmetic are to be continued through all three years; and each year is to close with a review and finishing course, devoting attention to individual needs.

4. Under the head of general administration the proponent urged the elimination of religious instruction in night schools, less attention to examinations for promotion, the prohibition of holding night schools in buildings occupied by children during the day, and careful inspection of night schools by appointed authorities.

Certain of these provisions were embodied in a ministerial decree of October, 1917, which stressed the importance of this branch of education in the national life, and appropriated $10,000 for the increase of the staff of teachers in commercial subjects and domestic arts.

Primary Education, Public and Private.

In 1917 slightly less than 100,000 pupils were enrolled in the 1,014 public primary schools of Uruguay, an increase of 2,500 over the preceding year. Of these, nearly 65,000 were enrolled in the city of Montevideo alone.

In administration and inspection the authorities in this field were active and progressive. Tentative reforms in the programs of study for the schools of towns and villages, a step long urged by them, were outlined by the minister of education; and wider latitude was allowed such individual schools in the matter of adapting nature study and practical courses to regular school work in accordance with local conditions and occupations. This step was in keeping with the attention paid to rural schools, which will be discussed later.

By executive resolution of July, 1917, the long-discussed change in the school year was made by which it shall hereafter open March 1 and close December 15. As with the similar change in Argentina, beneficial results, especially in the rural schools, are expected, as this arrangement is in conformity with climatic conditions. The change was made after investigation among the teaching force, and the country teachers won a victory over their city fellows, who favored vacations in the summer. This is but another and a significant effect of the steady centripetal attraction of the overshadowing capital city, more marked even in the new countries of South America than in the old ones of Europe. The country teachers have openly expressed their wish to spend the longest possible time in the capital, in spite of the inconveniences of such a sojourn in the summer. A further light upon the country teacher's point of view is shown by the information that the long vacations in winter permit the small landowner to employ his children in labors of battage, which begin in December and last most of the winter. The schools are therefore practically empty in winter. It is manifestly wiser to put the former long vacation of July at this time.

Complaints having become more frequent in regard to the blocking of educational administration in certain departments because of disagreements among inspectors, more drastic requirements were laid down by resolutions of the National Inspection of Primary Instruction, dated February, 1917. The authority of the departmental inspector over the subinspectors was confirmed; in the event of disagreement or insubordination the departmental inspector was required to present the case to the Department of National Inspection; the visitation of schools was distributed as nearly equally as possible; and the responsibility for inaction was put squarely upon the inspectors.

These provisions, rigorous as they were, did not prove adequate, and much of the business of the schools of the outlying departments still remained blocked. The executive, therefore, in November, 1917, transmitted to the Congress, along with a message emphasizing the necessity of the law, a project for the establishment of three divisions of regional inspectors of primary education to exercise general supervision over the departmental inspectors and the schools of the Republic. These regional inspectors acting as a unit were to constitute the technical inspection of the school authorities. Their functions were to be regulated by the executive in accordance with the reports of the national inspection and the general direction of primary instruction. The hitherto existing chief inspectors, technical, adjunct, and chief of statistics were to be transformed into regional inspectors, and under their immediate supervision were to be put all the departmental inspectors. The projected law encountered unexpected opposition, and its passage has not as yet been secured.

Scientific interest in the character of the textbooks adopted for use in the primary schools of Uruguay has been aroused by the Government's offer of prizes for satisfactory textbooks and by the publication in the Anales de Instruccion Primaria of illustrative lines and themes of treatment. The general assembly has authorized the offer of $6,000 in prizes in the contest for the composition of a book combining in a single volume all the textbook material needed in the fourth, fifth, and sixth classes in the public schools of Montevideo. This offer had as its object to lower the cost of education and thus to facilitate attendance, as the book in question was to be distributed gratuitously in cases of need.

A circular issued by the department of technical inspection in April, 1917, called the attention of teachers to the abuses of assigning written home work and limited such tasks to 30 minutes in classes of the first grade and to one hour for those in higher grades.

By executive decree, school savings funds and a system of aid for necessitous children, supplying clothing, midday meal, transportation, and books, were established and placed in charge of the administrative council for each department, composed of the departmental authorities of primary education, and the civil authorities of the several localities, presided over by the departmental inspectors. The funds for the institution of this system were to be drawn from State subventions to municipalities, school fees, and legacies and gifts to such objects. Although the Congress in October, 1917, appropriated $30,000 to organize the system, financial considerations have as yet prevented its practical organization.

Private instruction.—For the first time in the history of Uruguay systematic steps have been taken to ascertain the real nature and aims of private instruction. By executive decree of May, 1917, the inspector of private instruction and the assistant director general of primary public instruction were directed to address to every private educational institution in Uruguay a questionnaire in duplicate calling for information concerning its teaching staff, the mental and physical condition of its pupils, the hygienic conditions of the building and site, classrooms, dormitories, playgrounds, source and nature of drinking water, lighting conditions, school furniture and equipment, programs of study, methods, textbooks, school hours, and the general organization and administration of the school. No time limit was set for the reply, but it was requested within a reasonable time. The gist of the information gathered and the action of the Government have not as yet been published. Such a move has naturally aroused opposition in conservative and ecclesiastical circles, and its results are awaited with keen interest by other South American countries which have to deal with similar problems.

The issues aroused by the consideration of the private schools continued to grow more acute and culminated in the introduction of a bill in the Congress in March, 1918, forbidding the opening of private schools of any grade without the written permission of the inspectoral department of private instruction or the departmental inspectors of primary instruction; and requiring all teachers in private schools to hold a State teacher's diploma in accordance with the provisions of the law of public instruction, and debarring the clergy from teaching in any such private schools. The bill naturally became a storm center and is as yet unenacted into law.

Rural Schools.

Until the breaking out of the World War, and the consequent upsetting of traditions in all South American countries whose outlet is on the Atlantic Ocean, educational thought in Uruguay concerned itself largely with the capital city. In this respect, as in that of population (one out of three people in Uruguay lives in Montevideo), the centralizing tendency of South American countries is well illustrated. But a vital change began to show itself from 1914 to 1916, and in the latter year it acquired extraordinary impetus from the support of national leaders and of the press. The nation has grown steadily to recognize the proper balance to be observed between the claims of the schools of the capital and those of the rural districts. It has come to see that a healthy national life was possible only with organic changes in the schools of the outlying departments, and that these of Montevideo could without danger be left at their present status until the education of the people from whom the great city was steadily recruited should be attended to. It is in the light of this radical change in the national attitude that the educational history of Uruguay for the last biennium should be read.

This epoch in educational progress has been further marked by the recognition of the need of financial support for rural education, and the further need of differentiating the subjects of instruction proper for rural children from those adapted to the city. In getting this principle clearly before the public mind, the educational authorities of Uruguay have played a part excelled in few countries for skill and devotion to the national interests. Mention should be made of the able contributions of Señor A. J. Pérez, National Inspector of Primary Education, especially of his study entitled "De la cultura necessaria en la democracia" (Anales, 1918), which applies to modern conditions De Tocqueville's main lines of thought.

A commission of nine experienced teachers, six men and three women, with Señor Pérez as chairman, was appointed by executive decree to formulate the program of study for the projected rural schools. It began its sessions in February, 1917, and met frequently for two months. Its report was presented in May, 1917. Approved by the executive in June, by decree it went into effect on March 1, 1918. The main contentions of the commission in support of its plan are well worthy of notice:

1. Far-reaching changes within a generation in the commercial and industrial life of the nation have affected the rural districts and have called for different subjects and methods of instruction for the children of these districts. The rural school of the future must be recognized as fundamentally an elementary industrial school adjusted to local conditions.

2. The successful rural school must have the following aims: To inculcate conscientious and efficient labor; to minister to a well-regulated and happy home life; to diffuse the knowledge of private and public hygiene, and to further the increase of population and public wealth and, in general, the possession of a well-founded and enduring popular liberty.

3. The intimate relation of the rural schools with the problems of home life requires the new rural school to be taught by women, and therefore the training of young women as teachers in such schools should be at once initiated and continued as the basis of their success. Concrete illustration is found in the successful intensive training of 24 young women in a course of six weeks at the normal institute at Montevideo in the summer of 1917.

4. In the administrative organization the committee was guided by the following general principles: (*a*) Not to install rural schools by foundation or transfer except in localities where donations of ground of not less than 4 hectares (10 acres) should be immediately available; (*b*) to urge similar donations, public or private, to existing rural schools which lacked grounds of the minimum area above indicated; (*c*) to propose and encourage the transfer of rural schools that had no grounds annexed nor could obtain such by donation to another parish where such advantages could be obtained without prejudice to the interests of the rural schools in the district.

5. No child below 7 years of age should be admitted to the rural schools.

6. The programs of study for the rural schools occupied the greater part of the commission's time. The subjects of instruction as reported covered three years, and were reading, language work, writing, arithmetic, drawing, agriculture, domestic economy, elements of applied geometry, geography and history (local, national, and universal), singing, and gymnastics. In the view of the commission itself, the feature which peculiarly differentiates these new programs is the complete application of practical methods and aims to each of these subjects, the elimination of abstract and memory teaching, and, above all, the development of the subjects of drawing, agriculture, and domestic economy. The fundamental aim throughout was to correlate instruction with the conditions and occupations of life in the several communities and to lead the pupil to see each subject as related to practical utility.

Following the promulgation of the report of the commission, lively interest was manifested by the nation at large in the initiation of such rural schools. Practical difficulties, however, were foreseen in securing funds for their launching upon the nation-wide scale hoped for, and restlessness in certain quarters was manifested, though the Chamber of Deputies promptly voted the funds necessary. The National Rural Congress of Uruguay, in session in August, 1917, addressed to the minister of public instruction an urgent plea for carrying out the terms of the report in time for the opening of at least a part of such schools with the new school year.

Medical Inspection of Schools.

The medical inspection of schools has been favorably regarded in Uruguay for a number of years. It was initiated by law in 1913 with the examination of the pupils of the normal schools in Montevideo and the division of urban and rural schools into five groups. Since then popular approval of its application to the schools of the nation has steadily grown.

Under the present law individual inspection of the physical condition of pupils concerns itself only with those who enter for the first time. Naturally the law is applied with varying degrees of rigor, the schools of the capital being visited regularly by the medical inspectors, while those of the outlying departments are dependent upon the energy and faithfulness of the individual inspector. The law assigns to each a certain number of schools to visit. Capable medical inspectors have served their nation well in pointing out the grave disadvantages from the use of primary schools for night schools for adults, especially the danger of tuberculosis.

Medical inspectors are also required by law to include in their tri-monthly reports recommendations for repairs, alterations, etc., of school buildings and grounds called for by sanitary or hygienic considerations.

Dental inspection has also been systematically carried on in most of the schools of the capital, the reports of oral and dental affections observed in the children reaching 76 per cent of the total ailments noted. Ocular inspection in the schools of Montevideo has also been made a separate field within the last biennium.

By an amendment of 1916 to the existing law an annual physical examination of teachers in the schools of Montevideo will be required. This was naturally, and in certain instances bitterly, opposed; but the opposition has largely died down, and the teachers themselves have come to realize the benefits involved.

Physical Training.

In accordance with the wish of educational officials to diffuse among the schools of Uruguay the benefits of international progress in the physical betterment of school children, a commission was named by the executive in April, 1916, to draw up a plan of physical education in schools. This commission, acting in cooperation with the general direction of primary instruction, recommended to the executive the appointment of a permanent technical commission of physical training for schools, and this recommendation was approved by executive decree of March 8, 1918. The commission so appointed was to consist of a member of the general direction of primary instruction, one of the national commission of physical education, a physician of the medical school staff, a physician to be named by the National Council of Hygiene, the technical inspector of primary education, the technical director of the National Commission of Physical Education, the teachers of gymnastics of the normal institutes and of the primary schools of the capital, and two physicians who were specialists in diseases of children.

The province of the commission was to draw up for the general direction of primary instruction programs of physical exercises for schools; to outline methods of instruction; to see that these programs and methods were practically carried out in the public schools, to inform the school authorities upon points of deficiency in instruction and to indicate measures of correcting these; to organize gymnastic meetings and exhibitions for schools, and in general to promote the diffusion of physical education in the schools.

In furtherance of the awakened national interest in physical education, the executive has appointed departmental commissions in various departments for the immediate provision of adequate playgrounds and the acquisition of apparatus for games to be installed in town and village plazas. These have cooperated with the National Commission for Physical Education, the latter having decreed the establishment, upon application of residents, of neighborhood and community playing centers. All games, especially those of North America, which are adapted to the climate and environment have been systematically encouraged. In localities where it was required by law the executive has authorized the municipal authorities, with the consent of the national commission, to negotiate such loans as were necessary for the financial carrying out of this nation-wide scheme. These are steps of very great significance in a country of South America not by tradition or racial inheritance addicted to outdoor sports.

Secondary Education.

By executive message of February 14, 1918, the work of certain of the departmental liceos in discovering boys of talent in the higher elementary schools who were without means of continuing their education, and giving them opportunities to pursue their studies by means of a system of scholarships, was highly commended, especially as a beginning of bridging the chasm between elementary and secondary education.

In response to popular demand, courses in Italian and Portuguese were incorporated by decree of the secondary education division of public instruction in 1917. With the object of making known to teachers in secondary education the international progress in this field, a journal entitled "Revista de Enseñanza Secundaria" was established by executive decree under the direction of the secretary of this division. All reports and public business concerning this division are to be published in this journal.

By executive decree of November, 1917, all courses for the training of primary-school teachers maintained since April, 1916, in the liceos of the outlying departments were discontinued. They had been originally instituted by way of experiment for supplying teachers for the rural schools, and were not regarded as serving this purpose. Furthermore, in view of the agitation for improved rural schools, it was regarded as useless to continue a system of training which had proved, because of its environment, impracticable to harmonize with modern schools.

Commercial Education.

The past biennium has seen a considerable development of interest in commercial education. By executive recommendation and by law of January, 1916, there were introduced in the liceos and national schools of commerce in the capital and three of the larger cities courses of varying length for the training of boys for the consular, diplomatic, and foreign agency services. By ministerial decree of April, 1917, there were incorporated in the national schools of commerce courses in civil and commercial law, American history, and advanced courses in accounting and bookkeeping; and legal permission was given the individual school to extend the latter courses into the fifth year wherever deemed suitable. In common with students finishing the courses in the liceos, those from national school of commerce were granted opportunity to compete for scholarships abroad offered by decree of January, 1918. These scholarships are good for one or more years according to the success of the holder, and are apportioned among the departments according to the discretion of the council of secondary and preparatory education. Among the usual scholastic requirements called for are periodical reports from the holder of such a scholarship concerning the social and economic conditions of the people among whom he has been sent to study.

Following the plan drawn up at Montevideo in the summer of 1918 by governmental and educational representatives from most of the South American countries, invitations were sent to all interested in commercial education to attend the South American Congress of Commercial Education to be held in that city in January-February, 1919. The best talent in this division of education was assigned the discussion of topics which were considered as most urgent at the present time. They were treated under two main heads, those of (*a*) economic commercial expansion and (*b*) commercial instruction. The former head, not being essentially educational, calls for no notice here. The latter included the following topics:

1. From what points, how, and by what means commercial education should be developed on the American continent; extent and sub-division of such instruction.

2. Means of stimulating acquaintance among the peoples of the Americas.

3. The centers of commercial education as professional schools, and as

institutions of modern culture.

4. Should courses in business ethics be included in the curriculum of the advanced classes? Morale, character, and culture of students of commerce and of consular service.

5. Universal history of commerce as an indispensable element in the training of competent consuls.

6. Are screen films necessary in giving instruction in commerce and geography?

7. Countinghouse practice.

8. How should commerce be taught?

9. Teaching of languages in the centers of commercial education.

10. Preparation of women for a commercial career.

Among the resolutions officially adopted by the congress which had educational bearing were those recommending that—

(*a*) Institutes or sections of economic expansion in faculties of economic science, schools, and higher centers of economic and commercial study be established which should devote themselves especially to the study and practical solution of the various economic questions affecting inter-American relations and solidarity.

(*b*) For social and economic ends American countries create and aid industrial schools for fisheries and derived industries.

(*c*) Propaganda primers be prepared for exchange among the public schools of the (South) American Continent.

(*d*) There be included in programs of higher commercial study courses of comparative American economy and comparative customs legislation (the latter for consular courses), and that existing seminaries of economic investigation or higher commerce schools write the economic and financial history of their respective countries.

(*e*) The interchange of professors and students between the higher institutions of commercial learning be initiated.

(*f*) International agreements be concluded for the reciprocal recognition of degrees issued by institutions of commercial learning and that scholarships be granted for the interchange of students.

(*g*) The compilation of legislation of American countries concerning commercial education be intrusted to the permanent commission created by the congress. The commission will be assisted in this work by a committee of professors and experts in commercial education and will be charged with proposing plans and curricula in accordance with the following: Commercial instruction, which presupposes primary education, to be divided into three categories—(*a*) Elementary instruction, which may be dependent or independent; (*b*) secondary instruction; (*c*) higher instruction. The purpose of these branches is: (*a*) To train auxiliaries of commerce; (*b*) to prepare for commerce in general; (*c*) to furnish economic, financial, and commercial knowledge preparing for directive functions in commerce and industry, insurance and consular work, etc.

(*h*) Preliminary cultural studies of two grades be established, one confined to the first and second categories of commercial instruction, and the second for broader instruction in the third category.

(*i*) The study of the proposal of the National Institute of Commerce of La Paz, Bolivia, concerning education of women be referred to the permanent commission.

(*k*) Higher institutions of commercial education establish, if not already existing, in their curricula the separation of commercial from economic geography, the study of commercial geography to begin in primary schools, with periodical competitions for the preparation of the best commercial and economic geographies of each country and the exchange of prize works be arranged for.

(*l*) Institutions of bibliography and information be established, independent of or annexed to seminaries or institutes, for investigation existing or to be founded in America, and providing for the widest exchange of economic, financial, and commercial information collected.

(*m*) The practice of the professions receiving diplomas from higher institutions of commercial learning in commercial, civil, and administrative matters be legally recognized.

(*n*) An extraordinary prize to be known as the Pablo Fontaina Prize for Commercial Studies be offered for students of higher institutions of commercial learning. (Sr. Pablo Fontaina is director of the Superior School of Commerce of Montevideo and played a prominent part in the organization and work of the congress.)

(*o*) Entrance into consular and diplomatic services be granted by competitive examination or to candidates presenting degrees issued by official institutions of higher commercial learning.

(*p*) Courses of ethics in preparatory studies and lectures on commercial ethics in higher institutions of commercial learning delivered by distinguished professional men be established.

Training of Teachers.

Uruguay has always been progressive in this field. In 1914 Señorita Leonor Hourticou, the directress of the Normal Institute for Girls, submitted to the national inspector of primary instruction a far-reaching and systematic plan of reform in the aims and methods of practice teaching. She urged the establishment of a general directorate of teachers' practice training, composed of directors of normal institutes and the national technical inspector of schools, which body was to operate through a salaried secretary. Practice teaching for the first grade was to be required for one year with a minimum of 160 sessions and for the second year for at least three months with a minimum number of 60 sessions. Twelve schools for practice teaching were to be established at Montevideo. Local inspectors were to be appointed by the general directorate. While this scheme was not enacted into law, yet it had very great value in focusing the attention of the educational authorities upon the practical problem of reorganizing practice teaching.

These recommendations were allowed to lapse; but along with the demand for improved schools went a similar one for the improvement of the schools in towns and villages. In 1916 a committee of which the directress of the Normal Institute for Girls was chairman was appointed to formulate a training course for nonrural teachers which should be in keeping with the recognized needs of modern schools. In October, 1916, it presented as its report an outline of studies recommended to be incorporated in the three years' training course for primary teachers.

Taking up for the present only the teachers of the first and second grades, the committee recommended the following courses: Arithmetic, accounting, algebra, applied geometry, penmanship and drawing, elements of biology, zoology, botany, mineralogy and geology, anatomy, physiology and hygiene, physics and chemistry, studies in industries, geography and cosmography, history (national, South American, and universal), constitutional law, sociology and political economy, literature and composition, French, philosophy, and pedagogy with practice teaching. By the approval of the executive these courses were to go into effect in September, 1917.

Training of rural teachers.—The movement to improve the conditions of rural life which has been mentioned before began in earnest in 1914. In that year a report based upon an intensive study of the social and economic needs of the rural districts was presented to the general direction of primary instruction by a committee of teachers especially appointed for that purpose. Though no official action was taken at the time, the ventilation of the subject was very opportune and aroused public interest in a field so vital to the welfare of the nation. In every phase of rural education, and especially in the training of the teachers required, practical reforms were recognized as urgently necessary. From the strictly pedagogical point of view, the projects for teacher training as laid down in that report were of supreme interest, as constituting the basis upon which all subsequent suggestions have rested. They called for the establishment of a normal school exclusively for women rural teachers, which was preferably to be located either within the capital city or within easy access of it. This school was to work along the three main lines of agriculture, horticulture, and domestic science. For admission there was to be required, in addition to the usual certificates of mental, moral, and physical fitness, the certificate of completion of at least the third year of the program of the rural schools.

The courses were to cover at least two years, preferably three, with provision for four-year courses for pupils aspiring to the post of rural inspectors, an aspiration which was encouraged in the report. Only two or three scholarships were to be offered in each department, and the number of pupils was to be restricted to 50 for the first year. No purely theoretical instruction whatsoever was to be allowed. Increasingly specialized work in the practice school annexed was to be required of every pupil each year. For the last two years the work of practice teaching was to be so arranged as to alternate by semesters with the classroom work assigned. The latter, toward the end of each semester, was to review all the work from the beginning.

The projected institute was to be provided with all grounds, buildings, and equipment necessary for the teaching of every phase of rural life, including the care of fowls and cattle, with library and laboratories, with a modern gymnasium, with a hall for the teaching of the fine arts, and, most important of all, with a mixed practice school under the direction of the authorities of the institute, consisting of at least three grades and preferably four.

Summer courses for teachers, both men and women, were to be offered, emphasizing practical work in all courses related to rural life. Traveling schools of agriculture were outlined to appeal especially to youths of years beyond the rural school age and already engaged in farming, each class to have not less than 8 pupils and not more than 15, and to continue for periods ranging from one week to two months according to the demand in each locality. These traveling schools were to be organized for the same unit of territory as the rural schools already in existence. Each course was to be arranged in cycles as follows: (1) Three years' course in dairying; (2) four years' course in domestic science; (3) three years' course for rural teachers, men and women. Suitable certificates were to be awarded students satisfactorily completing these courses.

As regards the courses in rural schools, the committee found that the advantages accruing did not justify instructing pupils below 8 years of age in formal agriculture, satisfactory progress being made if the pupil was awakened to a love of nature and an interest in the life of the farm. Pupils above 8 were to be instructed in agricultural courses progressively adapted to their maturity and to the peculiar conditions of locality, soil, and climate.

As regards courses in domestic science, though the subject does not permit of a sharp age line of cleavage, yet the youngest girls might most profitably be given the elements, while the older girls might, in the discretion of trained teachers, take up the formal and technical study of food values in connection with elementary chemistry, physiology, and biology.

Anticipating the establishment of the normal schools for the exclusive training of teachers for the projected rural schools, the executive in November, 1917, sent to the Congress, along with the accompanying message, the project of a law for establishing two normal schools of agriculture in the Departments of Colonia and San Jose. These schools were intended to minister to the special need of these outlying departments. Their courses were to be intensive in character, adapted especially to the training of teachers for these localities, and to cover a year. Indeed, the bill specifically mentioned their purposes as intimately related with the forthcoming rural schools. The bill at once became a law, and the schools were to begin operation in March, 1918.

Higher Education.

In the field of university education no changes, administrative or instructional, are recorded for the past biennium; but there has been a certain amount of dissatisfaction with the administrative government of the University of Montevideo. In September, 1918, the executive sent to the Congress, along with an accompanying message, the project of a law clearly defining the constitution of the directive councils of the several faculties of the University of Montevideo as established by the laws of 1908 and 1915. Contention had arisen as to the right of electing representatives to each of these councils. By the new law each such council was to have 10 members and a dean. In the faculty of law four of these were to be elected by the attorneys who were also professors; four attorneys to be selected by those neither professors nor substitutes; one minor attorney by those neither professors nor substitutes; one student delegate by the students themselves.

In the faculty of medicine four members were to be elected by the professors, substitutes, and chiefs of clinics and laboratories; three members to be elected by the physicians not embraced in the above categories; one member to be elected by the pharmacists; and one by the dentists not included in the categories above; one member to be elected by the students of medicine, pharmacy, and dentistry.

In the faculty of engineering four members were to be elected by the professors and substitutes; three members to be elected by the engineers; and two by the surveyors who were neither professors nor substitutes; one member to be elected by the students of engineering and surveying.

In the faculty of architecture five members were to be elected by the professors and substitutes; four members to be elected by architects who were neither professors nor substitutes; one member to be elected by the students of architecture.

By decrees of 1917 enacted into law, seven years of advanced courses were required for the degree of doctor of medicine and five years for the degree of architect. Special courses of one and two years in construction and materials, leading to certificates but not to degrees, were formulated and allowed by the ministry of public instruction.

In pursuance of the policy of exchanging professors between the various countries of South America formulated at the Pan American Conference held at Buenos Aires in 1910, special exchange was arranged with Chile in 1916.

Education in Venezuela.

Primary education in Venezuela, during the biennium under consideration, has enlisted the practical interest of the National Government as never before. This has taken shape primarily in the two fundamental administrative decrees of the Provisional President, Dr. Bustillos. The first, issued in February, 1917, outlines the general requirements laid down in the organic law of public instruction under certain regulations for primary public schools. These are divided into three main heads: (*a*) The primary elementary schools, in which only those subjects belonging to compulsory primary instruction are taught; (*b*) higher primary schools, in which are taught the subjects belonging to higher primary instruction; (*c*) complete primary schools, in which instruction is given in both the above divisions at once.

The decree requires that each school be equipped with all modern appliances for the physical well-being of the pupils. Children are not admitted below 7 years of age; only those below 7 years are admitted to the mothers' schools or the kindergartens; only those above 14 are admitted to the schools for adults.

The subjects required in the elementary primary schools are: Reading, writing, and elements of Spanish; elements of arithmetic and the metric system; rudiments of geography and history of Venezuela; rudiments of ethics and civic instruction; rudiments of behavior and hygiene; the national hymn and school songs; the first elements of manual arts, and, for girls, of sewing.

In the higher primary schools are taught the following: Elements of Spanish grammar, elementary arithmetic, metric system, geography and history of Venezuela, elements of universal geography and history, elementary science, ethical and civic instruction, behavior and elementary hygiene, elements of drawing and music, manual arts and elements of agriculture and cattle raising for boys, sewing and domestic economy for girls, gymnastic exercises.

Religious instruction is imparted to pupils whose parents or guardians require it, provided that the number of such be at least 10. The celebration of school festivals as required by law, the establishment of libraries in each school accessible to both pupils and teachers, and the keeping of books and registers by teachers and directors are among the general provisions emphasized in the regulations.

The second decree, issued by the Provisional President in July, 1917, sets forth the regulations for the official inspection of public instruction. It expressly concerns the following schools:

1. Those maintained or aided by the Federal Union.

2. Those of primary, secondary, and normal instruction, maintained or aided by the States or by the municipalities.

3. Public and private schools satisfying legal requirements of good conduct and school hygiene.

The official inspection of schools has its ultimate authority vested in the following grades of functionaries:

1. Committees (juntas) constituted by law in localities maintaining a school.

2. Technical inspectors of primary, secondary, and normal instruction for the Federal District and the States of the Union.

3. A superintendent for the Federal District.

4. Inspectors necessary for the operation of higher and special instruction.

5. Commissioners appointed for special educational cases.

The duties and responsibilities imposed by law upon the juntas of primary instruction are detailed at greatest length, as upon them rests the proper execution of the law and the success of the entire system. Most important of all these duties are those pertaining to the enforcement of compulsory primary instruction. The juntas are required to keep themselves informed of the primary instruction imparted to all children of school age in their district, whether in schools public or private or at home; to require all parents and guardians of children of school age to have such children instructed as required by law; to keep themselves informed of the progress of all such children; to impose fines as required by law upon all parents or guardians who neglect the instruction of children; to see that the children admitted to schools of all grades conform in age, state of health, etc., to the requirements of the law; to visit the schools in their district frequently and regularly; and to keep registers of all facts pertaining to the attendance upon such schools.

The duties and responsibilities of the inspectoral juntas of secondary instruction and those of normal instruction are full and exacting and along the lines already laid down.

The technical inspectors as a group have charge of all three grades of instruction, each in the district assigned to him. As fixed by ministerial decree, there are 10 of these, excluding the superintendent for the Federal District. These functionaries are the direct agents of the ministry of public instruction, and form the connecting link between that office and the local juntas. They are vested with complete power to compel the execution of the law by the local juntas under penalties prescribed by law. They are instructed to work in complete harmony with the juntas, to call meetings, and to outline to them their duties under the law. They are also required to instruct teachers in their duties. In short, the inspectors are the element upon which the successful working of the machinery of the regulations depends.

The superintendent of public instruction in the Federal District is directly under the authority of the minister of education.

The inspectors of higher and special instruction have duties and responsibilities analogous to those of the inspectors already mentioned, though these, for obvious reasons, are not outlined at such length.

In the field of primary instruction the interest aroused in rural schools has been the most marked feature in the past biennium. The ministry of public instruction has paid special attention to the project of establishing rural schools, fixed or traveling, in the vicinity of the main manufacturing, industrial, or commercial centers of the country, and the President by decree of July, 1917, in commending the project, urged upon the juntas wherever possible to develop this type of schools. Especially in the agricultural or cattle-raising sections was the project received with enthusiasm, applying, as it did, directly to the problems of illiteracy and the training of the country population in practical subjects related to daily life. By special decree the President urged the introduction of elementary courses in agriculture in the established schedule of studies.

Among the States which definitely established such schools the State of Trujillo, fourth in population, took the lead by establishing 14, with predominant emphasis upon practical courses in agriculture and related subjects. Such schools began at once to serve as centers for the instruction not only of the children of school age but of the population generally in new methods, the use of machines, cooperative societies, etc. Similarly in sections devoted to cattle raising they were centers of inspiration and instruction in related subjects.

During the last biennium the industrial plants located in the centers of Venezuela have established primary schools for the children of their operatives, with the approval of the authorities, State and municipal. The minister of public instruction, in his memoria for 1918, urge upon the Congress the passage of a law recognizing the work of these schools, arranging for their inspection by the governmental technical inspectors and the classification and certification of pupils completing the courses offered in them. Such schools have also done much in combating the illiteracy among adults by means of night schools, and they have in many places, by employing excellent teachers, served the very useful purpose of raising the standard of requirement in various districts for the public schools, State or municipal.

Secondary education in Venezuela, according to the memoria referred to, suffers much from the insufficiency and irregularity of the revenues devoted to it, with the consequent inefficient equipment for modern and scientific subjects and the inadequate salaries of the teachers. On the pedagogical side the memoria found the effects experienced by secondary education from the mechanical and memory instruction, too largely prevalent in primary education, a permanent obstacle to any hope of real reform in secondary education.

The colegios, a type of secondary school peculiar to the Spanish-American countries, of grade preparatory to the liceos, seem to be disappearing from Venezuelan education. There are now left only 13 Federal colegios, all the others maintained by the States and municipalities having lapsed. The explanation probably lies in the exaggerated theoretical instruction they offered and its lack of adaptation to the actual needs of the nation. A number of them occupied buildings of some size and pretension, and the minister in his last memoria suggested that the vocational and industrial schools needed in the educational system might well be installed in these buildings.

Interest in the education of girls has made progress in Venezuela, an especially promising liceo for girls having been established at Caracas, offering advanced courses covering two years, with special attention to physical training and modern subjects.

Education in arts and crafts for men has long been popular in Venezuela, perhaps largely because of the national talent in those subjects. The school at Caracas, established in 1916, offers a four-year course, with English as the only foreign language. Within two years it reached an enrollment of 288 in the regular classes and 213 in the night courses.

Commercial education and training in political science courses have grown in popularity during the last biennium. Schools of the former have been established at Caracas, Maracaibo, Ciudad Bolívar, and Puerto Cabello; and of the latter, at Caracas, subsidized by the Government and regarded as an important adjunct in training for the legal profession.

In the field of the primary normal schools, the ministry has seen the necessity of their serving more largely the educational needs of the nation by supplying more and better teachers to the schools. It is, therefore, proposed to revise them thoroughly, especially in regard to the chief defect observed since their establishment, namely, the poor preparation of students who enter. It is proposed to offer, preparatory to the normal school proper, a perfecting course in essentials covering two or three years, to which would be added French, drawing, gymnastics, and music. Such a course would preferably be offered in the higher primary schools. The pupil should then proceed to the specialized subjects of pedagogy, methodology, psychology, and the history of education, these subjects to cover one year.

Another serious problem is the great difficulty experienced in securing suitable candidates for the scholarships offered in the primary normal schools by the several States and Territories. In many of them the memoria reports that the appointments had to lapse in view of the fact that no candidates qualified for them. The minister therefore suggested that a system of boarding departments, annexed to the normal schools, each accommodating about 20 boys of 10 to 13 years, should be established as feeders to the normal school system.

By presidential decree, dated July, 1917, special courses in practical agriculture, horticulture, floriculture, and domestic sciences were established in the primary normal schools, with the view of especially equipping teachers for the rural schools, whose establishment has come to be regarded as so necessary for the nation.

By presidential decree of March, 1917, an experimental station of agriculture and forestry, with an acclimatization garden, was established near Caracas. It is intended to serve as a model for other such stations in other parts of the country. "The objects of the station are the improvement of the methods of cultivation of the chief agricultural products of Venezuela; the introduction, selection, and distribution of seeds; experiments in reforestation; the suitability of soils to crops and of crops to various regions; and practical work for the training of agricultural foremen and forest rangers."

9 789361 382352

Printed by Libri Plureos GmbH in Hamburg,
Germany